EDGING TOWARDS DARKNESS

EDGING TOWARDS DARKNESS

The Story of the Last Timeless Test

John Lazenby

B L O O M S B U R Y
LONDON · OXFORD · NEW YORK · NEW DELHI · SYDNEY

John Wisden & Co Ltd
An imprint of Bloomsbury Publishing Plc

50 Bedford Square
London
WC1B 3DP
UK

1385 Broadway
New York
NY 10018
USA

www.bloomsbury.com

First published 2017

© John Lazenby 2017

www.wisden.com
www.wisdenrecords.com
Follow Wisden on Twitter @WisdenAlmanack
and on Facebook at Wisden Sports

British Library Cataloguing-in-Publication Data
A catalogue record for this book is available from the British Library.

ISBN: HB: 978-1-4729-4130-5
ePub: 978-1-4729-4129-9

2 4 6 8 10 9 7 5 3 1

Types   ices,

Printed an   CR0 4YY

To fi   )m.
Her   ng

To the memory of the fallen cricketers
of World War Two

Contents

Contents

A timeless Test match is played under no limitation of time and is designed to guarantee a decisive result. It is played until one side wins, however long that may take: hours, days . . . weeks. In theory, therefore, the timeless format eliminates all possibilities of a draw – the bane of international cricket played on the benign and often contrived wickets of the 1930s. As it has the luxury of time at its disposal, a limitless match is also meant to ensure that any interruptions for bad weather will not prevent a game from reaching its ultimate destination: a positive outcome. Unfortunately, timeless cricket was sometimes prone to failing its own test . . .

Introduction
When Time Ran Out

Norman Gordon, the last surviving man to play in a Test match before the onset of the Second World War, died peacefully in his flat in the Hillbrow district of Johannesburg on Tuesday, 2 September 2014, aged 103. Gordon was also the first international cricketer to reach a century in years and a last cherished link to the age of steamship timetables, eight-ball overs and tall scoring, in the language of the day; when batsmen gorged themselves on perfect wickets and bowlers, more often than not, fed off the scraps.

Once a thriving suburb of colonial villas, bookshops and cosmopolitan values, Hillbrow is now regarded as one of the most notorious neighbourhoods in the city: a hotbed of crime, poverty and squats; a world many times removed from that of the genial former Test cricketer, who was still practising as an accountant deep into his 93rd year. In the words of one writer, it is a place 'much closer to hell than the heaven it used to be'. But Gordon could not have moved away even if he had wanted to. The small flat he bought in the once fashionable Hillbrow, some 60 years earlier, would have cost more to sell than it was worth.

His good friend Ali Bacher, the former South African Test captain and cricket administrator who interviewed him for the television channel SuperSport shortly before his death, remembered an imperturbable character of strong personality, modest, engaging and always ready with a smile or a wry quip. Gordon refused to become a prisoner to his environment and told Bacher that all the time he lived in Hillbrow he never felt intimidated. 'There was only one occasion when he was bothered by someone at night,' Bacher informed *Cricinfo*, 'but in general everybody knew him there. He lived life to the full and was much loved.'

There was not much that could alarm a man who had seen and heard it all – from the cataclysm of world war, the rise of apartheid, his country's sporting excommunication, rehabilitation and subsequent regeneration, to the seismic shifts within the game he loved. He abhorred sledging, however – 'I never heard a dirty word uttered in my entire career' – and reminisced unashamedly about a time when kinship between opponents was an essential tenet of the sport.

Longevity was a recurring theme throughout his life. An avid golfer, he accomplished a hole-in-one at the age of 87 and played regularly until he was 96. As he explained once to *SA Cricket* magazine, with his customary gusto, he had no intention of spending his last days 'sitting in Hillbrow watching TV'.

Gordon succeeded the New Zealander Eric Tindill as Test cricket's eldest son after the hardy wicketkeeper-batsman passed away, aged 99, on 1 August 2010. A gifted all-rounder, Tindill also played rugby union for his country, winning a solitary cap at Twickenham on Saturday, 4 January 1936 in a match revered for two imperishable tries by the Oxford University undergraduate and Russian *émigré*, Prince Obolensky, and for England's first victory over the All Blacks. Years later Tindill confessed to smuggling the match ball off the pitch, tucked under his jersey on the final whistle, and returning to New Zealand with his prized trophy.

The young Gordon performed his own conjuring tricks with a ball. A right-arm fast-medium bowler who seldom tired, he was known as 'Mobil' for the handfuls of Vaseline he rubbed into his dark unruly hair, though on the pitch he was the antithesis of a showman. He possessed an equable temperament, along with a priceless ability to swing the ball both ways at a lively pace, and was rated by none other than

Walter Hammond as a bowler to bear comparison with the legendary Sussex and England seamer, Maurice Tate. Gordon preferred instead to compare himself to his countryman Shaun Pollock, whom he said he matched for pace and the similarity of their actions. In short, Norman Gordon of Transvaal was a captain's dream.

Yet, for all his undoubted qualities, he played only five Test matches for South Africa, all against Walter Hammond's MCC tourists of 1938–39, in a series pitched against the backdrop of impending war. The last of these, at Kingsmead in Durban, was timeless and is now universally acknowledged as *the* timeless Test. Weighing in at a prodigious ten days – the match stretched from 3–14 March 1939 and allowed for two rest days, while one day's play (the eighth) was lost entirely to rain – it is quite simply the longest Test ever played. A litany of records also perished in its wake and 'whole pages of *Wisden* were ruthlessly made obsolete'. If that was not enough one player, the fastidious South African batsman Ken Viljoen, felt the need to have his hair cut twice during the game. Extraordinarily, the contest had not been expected to last beyond five days – a distance that in all probability it might not have achieved, but for an unforeseen quirk of fate. Only the timeless games between Australia and England at Melbourne in

1929 (eight playing days), and West Indies and England in Kingston, Jamaica, in 1930 (seven days), come remotely close in terms of their durability, though the latter also ended farcically.

Timeless Tests are as old as the dawn of international cricket itself. Melbourne's Grand Combination Match, as it was billed in 1877, and later designated as the first Test match to be played between England and Australia, was limitless but consisted of only four-ball overs and concluded shortly before lunch on the fourth day. In fact, all Test matches played in Australia before the Second World War were timeless, and the format was an integral part of the country's cricketing culture for more than 60 years, before its inevitable extinction. In England, South Africa and the West Indies, timeless Tests were played only sporadically, where the concept was seen as nothing more than a last resort: a means of engineering a positive result if a rubber was all square or a side was one-up going into a final Test. England were leading South Africa 1–0 before the fifth Test at Kingsmead in 1939 and, as the series still remained alive, both sides agreed, under the conditions of the day, to play to a finish.

The Durban epic consisted of 43 hours and 16 minutes of playing time, yielding a veritable glut of runs – 1,981 – and 35 wickets from 5,447 deliveries, or 680.7 eight-ball overs. The new ball was taken a staggering 12 times. Norman Gordon contributed a back-breaking, sometimes heart-breaking, 738 balls (92.2 overs) to that aggregate, which remains to this day the most delivered by a fast bowler in a Test. His second-innings figures of one for 174 from 55.2 overs did not make for good accounting perhaps, but his long spells of sustained pace and swing – around the wicket, aiming into a worn patch on leg stump – deserved better and he still had the ball in his hand when, ironically and not a little embarrassingly, the timeless Test ran out of time.

Rarely can one cricketer have expended so much energy to a lost cause, though it is fair to say that 21 players – there was one exception – felt by the end as if they were all part of the same losing side. The Durban timeless Test was the last and, fittingly, the 99th of its kind to be played; and few could argue that it deserved to reach its century. However, the match remains vibrant with history and, in the age of immediacy when the future of five-day cricket has never looked so imperilled, it retains a fascination and an allure that is difficult to deny. There has even been talk of a comeback.

In July 2011 the International Cricket Council announced its plans for an inaugural World Test Championship. The tournament, which was scheduled to take place in England in 2013, would involve the four highest-ranked teams, two semi-finals, and a showpiece final at Lord's to determine the world champions. But what if five days of Test-match cricket failed to produce a winner? The ICC, it seemed, had a ready-made solution: a timeless final. In a press conference at Lord's, during which he appeared to be gloriously unaware of the elephant in the room, Haroon Lorgat, the then chief executive of ICC, declared that 'the final may be a timeless Test'. A South African of Indian descent, Lorgat continued, without a trace of irony: 'The committee is looking into the mechanics, but I would favour finding a winner because you need a world champion. It is not a good idea to end up with a drawn match . . .'

It is sometimes hard to believe that the ICC was serious about returning to a format that not only produced the stalest of stalemates in the history of the game, but prompted public outcry and a healthy dose of player power. One former player, Jack Hobbs, may have helped to win a timeless Test for England against Australia at The Oval in 1926, in tandem with Herbert Sutcliffe, but was now among its sternest critics. In his column in the London *Star* on 15 March 1939, he accused timeless Tests of 'killing the game' and could not resist noting that, 'Australia is the only country where they are popular.' But not just with Australians, it seemed. As the respected South African journalist

Louis Duffus, who imbibed the timeless Test's every ball, memorably put it, 'It was fantastic . . . the father of all Test match freaks.'

Not surprisingly perhaps, the World Test Championship did not come to fruition in 2013. The ICC committee failed to unravel the mechanics, the tournament was placed on indefinite hold and the timeless format returned to the shelf in the dusty box marked, 'Do Not Open.'

Yet the concept of a modern match with no time limits had not been without its enthusiasts when it was first mooted. In the *Independent*, the former England seamer Matthew Hoggard remarked that, 'It would be fascinating to see how the players of today would tackle a timeless Test. More and more games are finishing inside four days, and even inside three days in some cases, so would the tempo of batting change just because time was irrelevant?' The *Guardian* sports writer Andy Bull was similarly beguiled: 'It would be a wonderful tonic in a time of Twitter and Twenty20, Big Macs and Blackberrys.' The opinion that mattered, however, belonged to Norman Gordon. The timeless Test's only surviving participant was less than a month shy of his 100th birthday at the time and made no attempt to dilute his words. 'I bowled 92 eight-ball overs in the timeless Test, which equals 120 six-ball overs, to get just one wicket,' he was reported as saying when asked for his response. 'And I hope nobody has to go through something like that again.'

South Africa had adopted the eight-ball over in the Currie Cup competition of 1936–37, and the exertions of bowling flat out on a Kingsmead 'shirt-front', tailored to strokemakers of the quality of Walter Hammond, Len Hutton, Les Ames and Bill Edrich, to name but a few, remained indelibly etched on his memory.

Nonetheless, Gordon proved the pick of South Africa's attack by some distance and emerged, in the vaunted estimation of Hammond, as a bowler of 'striking potential'. His 20 wickets were more than any other bowler in the series and he pipped the great Yorkshire spinner Hedley Verity by one. He returned figures of five for 103 on his Test debut at the Wanderers in England's first innings, including the wicket of Hammond whom he dismissed on four of the seven occasions they opposed each other. In the opinion of William Pollock, the seasoned cricket correspondent of the *Daily Express* and the only national newspaper journalist to cover the tour (he was bylined to that effect), Gordon was 'the outstanding newcomer of the series'; he even included him in his notional World XI. 'He looks like being one of the bowlers cricket has been waiting for: another Maurice Tate.' The gimlet-eyed journalist spotted that Gordon polished only one side of the ball, leaving the other side rough – a trick, he believed, that accounted for his late and often abrupt swing. 'He has a great heart and we look forward to see what he makes of English pitches in 1940,' he reported, with what could have only been commendable optimism.

On Friday, 1 September 1939, barely six months after the timeless Test's untimely coda, Hitler invaded Poland, and two days later Britain declared war on Germany. Australia, New Zealand and India followed within hours, and South Africa joined the conflagration in a matter of days. As the South African wordsmith Duffus vividly phrased it: 'Many cricketers, from the veld and elsewhere, through six dark years, played the finest innings of their lives.' Some of those 'restless young men', he ventured, 'who, ten years previously, had lived on day dreams and hankered for travel, saw strange places they would never have included on their wander lists'. And some, of course, would not come home. The Englishmen Hedley Verity and Ken Farnes, and South Africa's 'Chud' Langton, all of whom contributed significantly to the timeless Test, just as they enriched and influenced every game of cricket they played, were grievous losses.

Gordon enlisted in the army, where he spent the war stationed at home and did not see action. But he did his bit, along with some 330,000 of his fellow countrymen for whom valour on the battlefield became a common theme. He returned to the Transvaal XI after the war but retired at the end of the 1948 season, leaving behind a tantalising glimpse of what might have been. Instead, he will always be celebrated as Test cricket's first centenarian and for shouldering the withering burden of 92 eight-ball overs through the timeless Test – a supreme feat of endurance for a bowler of his pace and wholehearted energy.

The humidity was so oppressive during those closing overs it felt as if someone had emptied a glue pot over him. The sweat saturated his flannels, he remembered, his shirt stuck to his back, and just running up to the wicket – he operated off a 'fairly long and easy' approach – required a marathon effort. He admitted later that he had been over-bowled. 'I was noted for my fantastic stamina and often bowled ten or 15 eight-ball overs at a stretch,' he told the *Daily Telegraph*. And all on a batsman's paradise: any blemishes on the Kingsmead 'shirt-front' were ruthlessly ironed out by the groundstaff, moving the South African batsman Dudley Nourse to recall how it 'sneered at the bowlers' throughout. This was the first Test series against England in South Africa to be played entirely on turf, the old coconut matting of previous tours having been finally jettisoned. Indeed, the wickets during the summer of 1938–39, at the Wanderers, Newlands and Kingsmead, were so plumb that they were referred to by one England batsman as being 'preposterously perfect'.

There is a photograph of the scoreboard of the timeless Test, taken after the final curtain, with England's second-innings total frozen for all time on 654 for five. It may not possess the glorious abandon of George Beldam's iconic portrait of Victor Trumper jumping down the track, nor capture the peerless authority of a Hammond cover-drive (a blue hand-kerchief curling from his hip pocket), as depicted by Herbert Fishwick's camera; but it is just as telling in its own way. The Kingsmead scoreboard is the recorder of a hundred images: the dwindling crowds, day by day; the ransacking of the record books; the immac-ulacy of the 766 deliveries sent down by Hedley Verity; Hammond completing his 21st Test century to equal Don Bradman's mark; the jarring juxtaposition of play ticking over at the pace of a grandfather clock winding slowly down, while Europe hurtled inexorably towards war; the black thunderclouds swooping low over Durban; the symbolic fading of the light; Gordon running in to bowl the 5,447th and final ball of the match.

That evening, on Tuesday, 14 March, the England party caught the 8.05 train out of Durban for the

1,000-mile journey to Cape Town, where the mail steamer, the *Athlone Castle*, bound for Southampton, strained at her moorings awaiting their arrival. Two days later they stepped onto the platform at Adderley Street Station into a world already tipping towards chaos: news of Germany's invasion of Czechoslovakia was splashed across every placard. It had been six months since Neville Chamberlain had purchased 'peace for our time' in Munich. Now Hitler was installed within the ancient battlements of Prague Castle – once the seat of the kings of Bohemia and the Holy Roman emperors – and cricket's longest day would soon turn to night.

One
Raking Over the Ashes

'No cricket match should occur again in which the wicket is contrived so that an innings of 900 is possible against any bowling' – Neville Cardus

Walter Hammond was appointed captain of England on Tuesday, 2 June 1938. The announcement that he would lead his country in the first Test of the summer against Australia was made during the England trial at Lord's, a game blighted by rain and freezing conditions. 'A screaming wind seemed to blow straight off the Polar ice,' Hammond – or more probably his ghost writer – lyrically recalled. As he had been invited to skipper an England XI against the Rest ahead of his two principal rivals for the job, the Middlesex pace bowler 'Gubby' Allen and the Warwickshire batsman Bob Wyatt (a third candidate, the all-rounder R. W. V. Robins also of Middlesex, did not even warrant selection at Lord's), the call came as no great surprise. Only the timing of it, midway through the game, raised a few eyebrows. Pelham Warner, the chairman of selectors, had almost certainly decided in advance of the trial that Hammond would lead his country in the first Test at Trent Bridge and could probably no longer keep up the pretence[1].

However, as if to disperse any lingering doubts, Hammond completed a century on the final day, despite being dropped four times before he reached three figures, and admitted he had been 'a mass of nerves' throughout his innings. One writer called it 'as laborious and painful a century as he ever made'. In the end, his elevation to the captaincy proved remarkably straightforward – for a man who spent the first 17 years of his playing career as a professional and had turned amateur only seven months earlier.

The cricket writer and historian Gerald Howat wrote of the times that, 'For a professional to captain a twentieth-century England side was unthinkable; for an ex-professional to do so was only barely tenable.' Yet Hammond crossed the social chasm of the tradesman's entrance to the front door, the work floor to the wood-panelled boardroom – he accepted a director's salary of £2,000 (worth almost £130,000 today) at the London-based firm Marsham Tyres – without so much as a stumble. More significantly the transition paved the way to the England captaincy, while allowing him to continue the lifestyle he craved. He was clearly ambitious for the job, though no more ambitious perhaps than Pelham Warner was for him, and the red carpet was effectively rolled out. He was granted membership of MCC and, within a few weeks of being entrusted with the England position, captained the Gentlemen to victory over the Players, becoming the first and only man to lead both sides[2]. The Gloucestershire captaincy passed into his hands the following season.

Outwardly, Hammond enjoyed all the trappings of an amateur. He liked expensive and fast cars, particularly Jaguars (he was the first cricketer, in 1929, to be given a sponsored car) and bought his suits from Savile Row; he liked to dress the part. Handsome and charming, when in the mood, he moved in glamorous circles, sought his friends outside of cricket and was not disinclined to brush up on his accent. He could also be socially uncomfortable and unsure of himself. He married the daughter of a wealthy Yorkshire wool textile merchant and attracted the kind of public adulation and celebrity more usually reserved for film stars of the day, acquiring a social status that went far beyond the aspirations of any professional cricketer. Indeed, some professionals were not above deferring to him as 'Mr Hammond' even before he turned amateur.

Inevitably, there had been some criticism of his appointment – much of it fuelled by snobbery, some of it directed at what was perceived as a lack of tactical acumen on his part, despite having shown himself to be a more than able captain of the Players. As for the men who had once been his former professionals, however, there were few quibbles, at least not publicly. Almost 50 years later Len Hutton wrote that, 'Hammond's captaincy was not highly regarded in some quarters, and, to some of his fellow players, he was inclined to be an aloof and Olympian figure . . . [But] to me, there could be no serious argument against his position as captain for he was comfortably the most talented player, with a wide experience.' When Hutton was offered the England captaincy in 1952, the class lines had converged to such an extent that, unlike Hammond, he could insist with all confidence on leading his country as a professional rather than an amateur. He remained, though, a fervent admirer of Hammond all his life: 'On the matter of his changing status from professional to amateur in order to take on the job, I had more sympathy for Hammond than for the prevailing system. He was not to blame for the way things were done in those days.'

The MCC side that toured South Africa under Hammond in 1938–39 also came to value his captaincy highly. He preferred to lead by example, with a bat in his hands, and rarely offered personal guidance or encouragement to his players; but he proved a popular leader, which was not always the case during his career. Hutton, Les Ames, Bill Edrich, Eddie Paynter, Norman Yardley and Ken Farnes were among those who spoke warmly and genuinely of his qualities, on and off the field in South Africa. Aside from the ever-present rumble of approaching war, it was a happy tour and one player above all others, Edrich, would owe his Test career to Hammond's nerve and keen judgment – and almost succeed in squandering it, too.

Hammond was only 17 days away from his 35th birthday when he accepted Pelham Warner's invitation to lead England against Australia. At an age when an international cricketer of today might be contemplating his retirement, Hammond was at the peak of his powers. On the field he was 'identifiable as a thoroughbred', his pristine whites, well-groomed appearance and blue handkerchief peeping from the pocket of his flannels as instantly recognisable as his sumptuous cover-drives. For some it was worth the admission fee alone just to watch Hammond walk out to bat. A fast-medium bowler, with a classical side-on action, he was good enough on occasion to take the new ball for England, though as Don Bradman remarked, 'He was too busy scoring runs to worry about bowling.' At slip he made the hardest catches appear ridiculously easy and, in his younger days, it was said, 'he threw like an Australian and fielded like an archangel'. A rare combination indeed. That Hammond was the obvious choice as captain, and head and shoulders above any other cricketer at the selectors' disposal, was not in doubt. 'A captain to the manner born,' the *News of the World* trumpeted in 1937.

When Hammond made his Test debut on the matting wickets of South Africa, aged 24, he was a devil-may-care batsman, willing, in the words of *Wisden*, 'to tilt at all the bowlers of the world'. During Percy Chapman's triumphant tour of Australia in 1928–29 he hit a record 905 runs in the series at an average of 113, quickly establishing himself as the most formidable player in the game and England's natural heir to 'The Master', Jack Hobbs. Yet within two years he had been trumped by Don Bradman, his record eviscerated – bettered by 69 runs – and trampled into The Oval dust, in a timeless Test that lasted six excruciating days. It was only the third timeless Test played in England, and Hammond's aversion to the format can perhaps be traced back to it. Although the young Australian lacked Hammond's elegance and grace, his brutal efficiency at the crease and almost machine-like devotion to scoring runs left the English public, and its cricketers, awestruck. His 'ugly determination', as Ken Farnes called it, with the heavy heart of a bowler.

From 1930 onwards Hammond engaged in a personal duel with Bradman, kindling 'a gladiatorial rivalry' between the two men that, despite being interrupted by war, would be maintained for nearly two decades. The England batsman Charlie Barnett, a former public schoolboy who played as a professional for Gloucestershire and didn't always see eye to eye with Hammond, claimed later that his desire to lead his country was piqued by Australia awarding the captaincy to Bradman in 1936.

As Hammond matured so his batting changed and, like Hobbs in 1919, he felt compelled to remodel his game. Gone were the more punitive strokes of his youth: he dispensed with the hook altogether and played more within himself, prepared to bide his time, to score as much off the back foot as he had once done off the front. It was a move attributable in part perhaps to his relentless and obsessive pursuit of Bradman. In the opinion of Neville Cardus he became a more calculating, thinking batsman, one who had 'put romance behind him', though not of course the

21

grandeur. Above all things, Hammond remained the supreme stylist.

It was to England's finest, and now captain, that the public turned during those troubled summer days of 1938 to provide some welcome distraction from the deafening headlines and threat of another war in Europe. And, anyway, the Australians were touring.

———

If the Test game of the 1930s was dominated by the battle for supremacy between its two pre-eminent batsmen, it was also a time of growth when the world of cricket spread its wings, extended its boundaries and broadened its horizons. West Indies, New Zealand and India, having joined England, Australia and South Africa in the magic circle of Test-playing nations, each toured Britain twice during the decade, influencing a shimmering new era of international cricket. To the names of Bradman and Hammond during the late thirties could be added those of Len Hutton, Denis Compton, George Headley, Learie Constantine, Stan McCabe, Bruce Mitchell, Dudley Nourse, Les Ames, 'Tiger' O'Reilly, 'Chuck' Fleetwood-Smith and Hedley Verity. Test matches in England were usually scheduled over three days (unless the Ashes were at stake, when four was the standard) and played infrequently enough to sustain their popularity and freshness in the face of growing competition from other sports. Even the game between MCC and the Australians at Lord's, played in May of 1938, drew a crowd of 32,000 on the opening day, and the gates had to be closed by early afternoon.

But it was not only cricket that flourished in England. In 1934 the professional golfer Henry Cotton (whose first love just happened to be cricket) ended almost ten years of American hegemony by winning The Open at Royal St George's; he repeated the trick in 1937 and again in 1948. Fred Perry, meanwhile, claimed three consecutive Wimbledon singles titles between 1934–36, confirming his status as the No. 1 player in the world and reviving in the process the good name of British sport. Worcestershire's Dorothy Round kept him company, winning the women's title in 1934 and 1937. In football, Stoke City's Stanley Matthews earned the sobriquets 'The Magician' and 'The Wizard of Dribble', and centre-forwards Tommy Lawton and Ted Drake, of Everton and Arsenal respectively, knocked in goals for fun – the latter frequently profiting from the trickery and unerring left foot of Denis Compton. The man who would become the most dazzling batsman of his generation was also fêted as the best outside-left in England, his sorcery often compared to that of Matthews.

The thirties were not always so promising, however. Britain's decade had started under the grim shadow of the Depression, or the Great Slump as it was known, when unemployment ran as high as 2.5 million by the summer of 1932. Cricket was not immune to the crisis, though most county professionals could count themselves profoundly fortunate that, unlike many of their fellow workers, they still drew a wage. Some counties, such as Worcestershire, felt the pinch more than others and had to resort to fund-raising appeals. But at a cost of a shilling (or sixpence after the tea interval) county cricket was cheap to watch and, in the words of Gerald Howat, remained 'a pleasant way to while away the hours of enforced idleness'.

The economic recovery was at least swift and, despite the fact that the industrial north of England and much of Scotland, Wales and Northern Ireland were still overwhelmed by a dire shortage of jobs and food, the Chancellor Neville Chamberlain felt sufficiently confident in 1934 to inform the Commons: 'We have finished the story of *Bleak House*, and are sitting down this afternoon to the first chapter of *Great Expectations.*' And so began the age of 'the pictures' and matinée idols, the aviation and the automobile industries – when Humbers, baby Austins and the 'bullnose' Morris took to the roads – of television, swing jazz, Art Deco wireless sets, the

Lambeth Walk, washing machines, Littlewoods
football pools, greyhound racing, Billy Butlin's
holiday camps, flannel 'bags', Bakelite sunglasses, and
the long shadow of war.

———

Don Bradman's Australians docked at Southampton
on 20 April for what turned out to be the last Ashes
series for eight years. It was Bradman's third tour
of England and, in another bravura display of
batsmanship, he not only passed 1,000 runs before
the end of May, for the second time, but registered
centuries in three of the Test matches in which he
went to the wicket – at Trent Bridge, Lord's and
Leeds – to become the first man to average over a
hundred in an English season. The third Test at Old
Trafford was washed away without a ball being
bowled, while an injury prevented him from batting
in either innings at The Oval.

At Trent Bridge in Hammond's first match as
captain, played on what many regarded as the most
perfect batting wicket they had seen, records tumbled:
England exceeded their highest total against Australia,
reaching 658 for eight declared, and Lancashire's
Eddie Paynter struck an unbeaten 216, the best score
by an Englishman against Australia in England – a

record that would stand for barely two weeks. There were centuries, too, for Hutton and Compton on their Ashes debuts. When Australia batted Stan McCabe eclipsed them all with 232, an innings so exhilarating that Bradman ordered all his players onto the balcony to watch, insisting that they might never again see an exhibition of such power and presence. He was eventually dismissed by Hedley Verity, though Hammond's reluctance to give his premier spinner no more than seven overs while McCabe had been in full flow drew some stinging criticism in the newspapers. England's new captain enforced the follow-on, but the obligatory Bradman century – 'the hardest of his career', according to one reporter – saved the game. The second Test, at Lord's, also made history when it became the first to be televised live.

Television had flickered into life in 1936, and the BBC's outside broadcast cameras had already been present at the Boat Race and at Wembley for the FA Cup Final of April 1938. The Cup Final was contested between Huddersfield Town and Preston North End, who included a young Scottish wing-half by the name of Bill Shankly, and watched by a crowd of 93,497. It was a game of northern grit and heft, and would be remembered primarily for commentator Thomas Woodrooffe's infamous gaffe in the closing moments. The scores were deadlocked at 0–0 after 29 minutes of

extra-time when an exasperated Woodrooffe informed
the viewers in his brisk, clipped tones: 'If there's a goal
scored now, I'll eat my hat.' Seconds later George
Mutch was flattened in the box; Preston were awarded
a penalty and the inside-forward climbed slowly to his
feet to drill the ball in off the underside of the bar[3].

Initially, there had been concerns that television
coverage at Lord's might reduce the attendance figures
but they proved unfounded. Only 5,000 people
owned a television set in 1938, while millions more
lived too far from the transmitter at Alexandra Palace
in north London for it to matter, and the spectators
streamed through the turnstiles in their thousands.
Thousands more had to be locked out of the ground.
'This was Lord's in June, with London spread around
us,' Neville Cardus lovingly observed in the *Manchester
Guardian*. 'If Hitler could have looked upon the scene
probably he would have said, "Still kicking the cricket
ball about."' And there was something else to stir
Cardus's imagination: 'Gaunt contraptions reared to
the heavens, devices of television, broadcasting.'

When Hammond walked to the wicket on the first
morning with England 20 for two, soon to be followed
by 31 for three, the huge crowd might have feared the
worst. But by the close he was 210 not out, and any
concerns that his scoring powers would be affected by
the burden of captaincy had been conclusively erased.

He added a further 30 runs in 32 minutes the following morning in front of a record Lord's crowd of almost 34,000, before losing his leg stump to the fast bowler, Ernie McCormick. Hammond had spent six hours at the crease in all, and the crowd stood and cheered him all the way back to the pavilion. It was his crowning moment, 'a throne-room innings', as Cardus soliloquised, when 'more handsome cricket could not be imagined'. For once even Bradman was upstaged but, frustratingly for England, the game ended in another draw.

———

By the time the sides reached The Oval for the fifth Test in late August (where the television cameras were once again in place), Australia had retained the Ashes, triumphing by five wickets amidst the pinballing emotions and rolling thunderclouds of Headingley. Bradman remembered the fourth Test as 'the greatest of modern times', and for 'the darkest [conditions] in which I have ever batted'. More extraordinarily, he recorded his sixth century in successive Tests, and was rivalled blow for blow, ball for ball by 'Tiger' O'Reilly, who spun his leg-breaks venomously and was the catalyst for a spectacular England collapse in which nine second-innings wickets fell for 63 runs, including that of Hammond. The cheers for the England captain's arrival at the wicket had died almost instantaneously after he turned his first ball, a quick googly from O'Reilly, to short-leg and was caught low down and one-handed by Bill Brown; with his departure went the Ashes. The series, however, still remained alive and, as England had a chance to square the rubber in the final Test of the summer, the timeless option was brought into play at The Oval.

It soon became known as 'Hutton's match'. Hammond won the toss for the fourth time in a row and the 22-year-old opening batsman occupied the crease for nearly 14 hours, compiling an astonishing 364, before his captain finally called a halt at 903 for seven on the third day. For the third time that summer the palm for the highest individual score by an Englishman against Australia in England changed hands. Hutton claimed later he received no specific instructions from Hammond on how to pace his innings, though he recalled that after driving O'Reilly over mid-on, having reached 140, the England captain appeared on the players' balcony and 'quickly made clear my role to me, signalling his orders to cool it. I wouldn't be permitted any attacking luxuries'.

Hammond declared only after injuries to Bradman – who fractured his shin bone while bowling his occasional leg-breaks – and Jack Fingleton, with a severely strained leg muscle, had reduced the tourists to nine batsmen. The naturally suspicious Hammond even sought medical advice to confirm that Bradman was unfit to bat. Otherwise he might have been tempted to exceed a thousand runs on a wicket that The Oval groundsman, 'Bosser' Martin, had boasted would 'last until Christmas'. Some clever wag even attempted to calculate what effects snow might have had on the surface. In the end the match did not even scrape into a fifth day, despite Martin's pluperfect pitch.

Hutton, 160 not out at the close on Saturday, spent the rest day relaxing by playing beach cricket at Bognor Regis in the company of his Yorkshire soulmate and 'faithful ally', Hedley Verity. When play resumed he simply carried on where he had left off, calmly ticking off the records as he went: Hammond's 240 at Lord's, R. E. Foster's 287 at Sydney in 1903, Bradman's 304 at Leeds in 1934, Andy Sandham's 325 against West Indies in Kingston, Bradman's 334 in 1930, again at Leeds (an innings Hutton had watched spellbound as a 14-year-old schoolboy), and Hammond's 336 against New Zealand at Auckland in 1932. All were surpassed.

Eventually, he was caught in the covers off O'Reilly, beaten by exhaustion more than anything. The newspapers waxed lyrical, even the American press thought it worthy of a mention. Among the flood of accolades for the Yorkshire prodigy, the *Daily Express* exclaimed: 'England finds her Bradman.' Many believed that England had already found her Bradman in the form of Walter Hammond. Yet, for all his princely talents, Hammond's fate – one that rankled miserably with him – was to spend much of his career batting in Bradman's slipstream. Still, The Oval gave him his first victory as England captain and one to savour; even Chamberlain and Hitler briefly ceded prominence on the front pages. The Australians were routed for 201 and 123, losing by the staggering margin of an innings and 579 runs. Perversely, the Australian Board of Control had spent the days before the game voicing its objection against four-day Tests and promoting a campaign for all future Ashes contests to be played to a finish.

In fact there were already signs that the clock was ticking for games with no time limit, though few in the crowd, basking in the sunlight of England's victory, could have guessed they had just witnessed the penultimate timeless Test – despite its many distinguished critics. Howard Marshall, the BBC broadcaster and the first voice of cricket, wrote in the *Daily Telegraph* that the match was 'a trial of endurance', where 'real cricket was knocked out by the wicket which was so unhelpful to the bowlers that batting was largely a matter of patience and stamina'. *The Times* took a similar view: 'the affair [was] reduced to a run-making competition and bowlers were regarded essentially as a luxury'. Cardus, who made no effort to disguise his distaste for timeless cricket, reserved his sympathies for O'Reilly, 'the best bowler of the age, [who] laboured alone on the lifeless hearthrug'. 'Chuck' Fleetwood-Smith, who might easily have been described as the second best bowler in the world, fared no better with his left-arm googlies, and his figures made for grisly reading: 87-11-298-1. 'The wicket prepared for this engagement was unfair to skilful bowlers and not in the interests of cricket,' Cardus added, and laced his words with the warning: 'No match should occur again in which the wicket is contrived so that an innings of 900 is possible against any bowling.'

Such impressions counted for little among Yorkshiremen everywhere, or with the thousands of joyful spectators who had crammed into every available space at The Oval to roar Hutton towards the 300-milestone – an achievement that was greeted with at least a minute's standing ovation. The young professionals Hutton and Compton were the gilded duo, the brilliant new stars in the batting firmament, heralding a bold and exciting future for English cricket. Whatever that future might be. England were scheduled to tour Australia again in 1940–41, but nobody was daring to think too far ahead.

———

By the end of the summer, government depots had been opened for the distribution and fitting of gas masks, and the sight of shelter trenches in London parks, city landmarks surrounded by sandbags, and office windows painted black, heightened the grim inevitability of war. The signing of the Munich Agreement on 30 September sent a brief but palpable surge of relief through the country. Chamberlain, who had succeeded Stanley Baldwin as Prime Minister a year earlier, returned to Heston Aerodrome to a hero's reception, brandishing the piece of paper on which he had secured the signature of Adolf Hitler: 'peace for our time'. But, as many feared, the pact proved to be no more than that – paper-thin – and brought only a temporary postponement of war, though one that was long enough to allow Britain to rearm.

Two days before Chamberlain's triumphal home-coming from Munich, Bradman left England bound for Australia. He was taking a detour through France to Toulon (against the advice of his travel agent), where he would catch up with the rest of his team who had already sailed from Tilbury. There had been suggestions that the Australians might sail for home via the Cape, rather than the Mediterranean, in case war broke out while they were at sea. 'My greatest impression is of the magnificent calm and spirit of our British people during these last troublesome days,' Bradman told the press on his departure. 'I know we all fervently pray for peace.' He had only recently celebrated his 30th birthday and his position as the No. 1 batsman in the world was irrefutable. In addition, Cardus observed during The Oval Test that, 'His fielding and his eager and sensible captaincy were beyond praise; he nursed his bowlers, talked to them, put his arms in theirs between overs, and cheered them up; he was not only the team's captain but the father-confessor and philosopher.'

That would never be Hammond's style of leadership (some would argue it was not Bradman's either), but his reappointment as captain of MCC for the winter tour to South Africa was a mere formality. He had triumphantly vindicated Pelham Warner's championship, and the decision was confirmed on 27 July. Many, in fact, felt England were a better equipped all-round team than Australia, and MCC's selection perfectly reflected the growing strength of the English game; with its judicious blend of youth and experience, it was considered superior to any that had visited South Africa before. The selectors could even afford to leave behind The Oval centurions Maurice Leyland

and Joe Hardstaff along with the Yorkshire yeoman Bill Bowes, who had provided admirable support for the decidedly rapid but inconsistent Ken Farnes of Essex. The most notable absentee was Denis Compton, who was under contract to play for Arsenal, the reigning First Division champions, during the 1938–39 league season. The Gunners, as epitomised by their new, sleek Art Deco stadium at Highbury, were the powerhouse of English football – a club that had succeeded in having the name of the nearest Tube station changed from Gillespie Road to Arsenal – and were determined to keep their man.

Nonetheless, with Hammond, Hutton, Paynter, Edrich and the graceful Kent amateur Bryan Valentine – a batsman imbued with an abundance of confidence and adventure – in the vanguard, England would not lack for runs in South Africa. Cambridge University and Yorkshire's Norman Yardley, a future captain of his country, and Sussex's Hugh Bartlett represented the new intake of batsmen. A compulsive strokemaker and protégé of Frank Woolley, the left-handed Bartlett had already alerted the Australians of his ferocious hitting power, hammering the fastest century of the season off them at Hove in only 57 minutes. 'It produced a spectacular contrast for the tourists, who had just had to field out to Hutton's 364 at The Oval,' *Wisden* noted. The Kent wicketkeeper

Les Ames added substantially to the batting riches, while his understudy Paul Gibb (another Yorkshireman and Cambridge blue), though not first choice with the gloves for his county, was also an accomplished run-maker[4].

The pace bowling would be shouldered by the strapping 6 foot 5 inch Farnes and Worcestershire's uncapped Reg Perks, a highly effective and consistent performer who could produce spells of genuine speed. In a trade that was almost exclusively the preserve of professionals, Farnes remained that rarest of beasts – the amateur fast bowler. Although he was considered the quickest in England, or indeed anywhere for that matter, he tended to be governed by his moods. 'He was either destructively hostile or complacently amicable,' *The Times* wrote. There were times when he needed to be goaded into action, but 'in his full fighting feathers', the newspaper added, 'he was a danger to any batsman in the world' – the heir, in terms of pace, to another great amateur and man of Essex, Charles Kortright, a scourge of Victorian and Edwardian batsmen.

Hammond and Edrich could be relied on to supply valuable back-up to the strike bowlers. Indeed, Edrich was capable of bowling genuinely fast, generating steep bounce from a low, slinging action, despite being no more than 5 feet 6 inches tall. 'Explosive' and 'tearaway' were epithets regularly applied to his bowling, as Cardus evocatively put it: 'I expect to see dust and newspapers eddying in the air whenever he bowled fast – like the tremendous atmospheric disturbance which happens on a railway station platform as an express train thunders through.'

More emphasis had been put on England's spin attack, led by the left-arm Hedley Verity, the prematurely greying nonpareil of his craft. He would be joined by two leg-spinners, Doug Wright and Len Wilkinson, and the off-spinner Tom Goddard. Unusually, Verity, Wright and Goddard had all started life as seamers, before turning their hands to spin in the knowledge they lacked that vital commodity, extra pace. Goddard still displayed the characteristics of his former trade, notably when appealing for lbws in a booming bass, while Wright bowled his googlies and leg-breaks at a brisker pace than any other wrist-spinner, O'Reilly included. Verity's bowling style was frequently described as slow-medium, and he used his height (almost 6 feet) to obtain sharp lift and turn. The Lancastrian Wilkinson had propelled himself into the selectors' thoughts with 151 wickets in his first full season, and the world lay before him. A South African proposal that the wickets be covered during the Test series, thereby restricting the effects rain might have in spicing up the surface, had been roundly rejected by MCC, and the spinners could expect to get through a mountain of overs on tour.

There was no vice-captain, though Yardley, already being groomed as Hammond's successor, would lead the team in his absence. Flight lieutenant Jack Holmes, the debonair Sussex captain and middle-order batsman, was appointed manager and would be a more than useful replacement in the event of injuries. Goddard, at 38, was the veteran of the party and Wilkinson – Hutton's junior by only five months – the tenderfoot, at 21; their average age was 27. The full squad was: W. R. Hammond (captain), T. W. J. Goddard (both Gloucestershire); L. Hutton, H. Verity, N. W. D. Yardley, P. A. Gibb (Yorkshire); E. Paynter, L. L. Wilkinson (Lancashire); L. E. G. Ames, B. H. Valentine, D. V. P. Wright (Kent); K. Farnes (Essex); W. J. Edrich (Middlesex); H. T. Bartlett (Sussex); R. T. D. Perks (Worcestershire).

On Friday, 21 October the 15 MCC cricketers caught the boat train from Waterloo Station to Southampton, where they would board the Union-Castle Line's *Athlone Castle* for the two-week voyage to the Cape. When they assembled in London, amidst the jostling crowds and flashing camera bulbs of the press, there was the unmistakable aura of adventure that accompanied any long sea voyage or train journey. Yet, as Edrich wrote, most of the players had mixed feelings: 'The prospect of cricket and travel ahead of us was delightful; but we all felt anxious about political events and were conscious that war might break out at any time during our absence, despite the Munich Agreement and the subsequent pretty speeches.' For the shy Hutton, who had barely had a day to himself since becoming a record-breaking celebrity (though judging a beauty contest at Butlin's Skegness holiday camp was hardly a chore), the four-month tour to South Africa must have seemed like an escape. He was 'ready for a new world and a change of scene'.

At Waterloo the press had greeted him with cries of 'Where's 364?' – the name given to the Gradidge bat with which he scored his runs at The Oval. The bat had been insured and was already on exhibition in South Africa, awaiting the team's arrival; another four, he explained, were safely stowed in his luggage. Once again he was besieged by hundreds of autograph hunters, and several jumped onto the footboards of the train as it moved out of the station, thrusting their books at him through the window. They were joined on the footboards by a telegram boy who had sprinted down the platform, waving a batch of golden-coloured envelopes containing last-minute messages of good luck. The *Daily Express* even ran the headline,

'Girls mob players', above a photograph of a beaming Hammond and Valentine, looking more like city businessmen in their double-breasted pin-stripe suits. A supplementary headline asked: 'Will they come back smiling?'

Two

The Rise of the Springboks

*'We were conscious of the fact that we represented
nothing like the threat to the supremacy of English
cricket that an Australian side does' – Dudley Nourse*

South African cricket came of age on 2 July 1935
when, after 28 years of almost persistent struggle, it
secured a first Test triumph in England. The margin
of victory by 157 runs could not have been more
emphatic, coming against an England side that
included Hammond, Sutcliffe, Leyland, Ames and
Verity. Nor was there a more exalted place in which to
achieve it than at Lord's. The young batsman Dudley
Nourse, who was on his first tour to England, admitted
to finding London 'rather frightening on first
acquaintance, with its unbelievable bustle and crowds',

but Lord's was simply overpowering. 'The world seems to be left outside and here inside is a new world,' he reflected after venturing through its gates for the first time. 'It is like coming into a temple and being confronted by a beautiful shrine.' Not surprisingly perhaps, in only his second Test, Nourse was unable to leave his mark on the occasion and was bowled by the hard-headed Verity in both innings, mustering just five runs.

The eighth South African team to visit England, under the fearless captaincy of Herbert Wade, were a popular and good-natured band who, *Wisden* noted, 'drew crowds far above the number expected wherever they went'. They also confounded expectations, both in England and at home, winning 17 of the 31 first-class games they played and losing only two. The first of those defeats came as late in the tour as 13 August, against Gloucestershire, by which time their reputation was assured. Gone were the days when they might be rattled out for 30, as they were by Maurice Tate and Arthur Gilligan in only 75 balls in a Test at Birmingham 11 years earlier. The key to their striking improvement could be traced back to the gradual transition from matting to turf wickets, a policy that had been under way since the end of the 1920s. As a result, *Wisden* recorded, 'The players, when they arrived here, did not have to learn – or unlearn – so much as their predecessors and this 1935 side held a pronounced advantage compared with previous South African teams visiting England[1].'

The architects of the Lord's victory were the wondrously named leg-spinner Xenophon Balaskas – who bowled on a dusty wicket that might have been fashioned for him – the second-innings centurion Bruce Mitchell, and the wicketkeeper-batsman 'Jock' Cameron, who hit 90 at a giddy rate to revive South Africa's fortunes after they had been reduced to 98 for four on the first morning. But it was the opening bat Mitchell who proved the revelation, hitting the ball to all parts of the ground with strokes that few suspected he possessed. South Africa had started their second innings with a lead of 30 and the game hanging in the balance. Apart from the involuntary Mitchell mannerisms – the nervous tugging of the gloves, the continual touching of his cap and collar – he was unrecognisable from the batsman who glorified in defence and chipped his runs out of tablets of stone.

'It was Mitchell's masterpiece,' Louis Duffus wrote, 'an innings with a rich quality of genius.' Remarkably, for such a prolific run-scorer, he was uncomfortable batting in front of big crowds and never lost his acute shyness. 'I would wager that he blushes every time he is singled out for applause by an enthusiastic crowd,' Duffus added. Mitchell was not without a dry sense of humour, though. The slowest of slow leg-spinners who bowled off only one pace, he was asked once for his views on the introduction of the eight-ball over and replied that he would have to cut his run down.

He had been struck over the eye by the ball in the game before Lord's and played in the Test with stitches and a plaster protecting the wound. His participation had been in doubt before the start and he appeared in some discomfort during both innings. Yet when Wade declared South Africa's innings at 278 for seven, setting England 309 to win in just under five hours, Mitchell was undefeated on 164, having reached the highest score by a South African in England. C. B. Fry, in the *Evening Standard*, announced with a magisterial turn of phrase that Mitchell batted 'like the schoolmaster of all bowlers ever born'. Nonetheless, Wade's declaration was adventurous and relied on Balaskas reprising his form from the first innings, when he spun the ball alarmingly at times and propelled his googlies at a waspish pace. The captain kept his leg-spinner going for almost three hours from the pavilion end, and with the versatile 'Chud' Langton in support, employing a potent mix of seam and spin, the gamble paid off: England were bowled out for 151 at five o'clock on the third and final day. Only Hammond and Sutcliffe put up a fight.

Fittingly, Balaskas captured the last wicket, luring his fellow leg-spinner, the No. 11 batsman Tommy Mitchell, out of his crease with the final ball of his 27th over. It curled past the outside edge and Cameron removed the bails in a blur. Whereupon, Duffus reported, the wicketkeeper was 'like a reaper gathering up a wheatsheaf, he wrapped his arms in embrace round the stumps and bolted off with his precious souvenirs'. Balaskas finished with four for 54 and match figures of nine for 103.

The son of Greek migrants who owned the first restaurant in the diamond mining town of Kimberley, Balaskas was one of Test cricket's more intriguing characters. A chemist by profession – naturally, he was dubbed the 'Greek Chemist' during his playing days – he bounded in off a short run and bowled with wit and invention in an era replete with wrist-spinners. He was also a more than handy batsman, who took a Test century off New Zealand in 1932. On the eve of the Lord's Test he and Duffus had been strolling near Leicester Square when they chanced upon Greek Street, in the heart of Soho. The little leg-spinner considered it a lucky omen and, with the magical sound of American jazz filling the night, innocently persuaded his companion to explore the neon-splashed street with him. They wandered past the rows of restaurants, pubs and clubs, politely ignoring a chorus of 'hullo, boys' from every doorway, before hurrying on their way. Omen or not, Balaska never again produced bowling to match his figures at Lord's.

———

Faced with the deflating prospect of a third successive series defeat (they had lost to Australia the previous summer and West Indies in the winter), England did everything they could to exact a result in the third and fourth Tests at Leeds and Manchester, and South Africa everything they could not to lose. Both games were drawn, though not without a few alarms for the tourists, and it all came down to the final Test at The Oval, as it so often did. The England captain Bob Wyatt won the toss and, in a high-risk strategy, put South Africa in on what looked to be a perfect batting strip. Wyatt gambled on the moisture in the surface assisting his fast bowlers early on to provide England with their best chance of squaring the rubber. But the Springboks did not lose a wicket until the afternoon session, by which time the gamble had backfired.

Mitchell, having revealed the hidden side to his batting at Lord's, simply reverted to type and scored a typically defensive century, occupying the crease for almost five hours. There was a hundred for Eric Dalton too, batting as low as No. 8, and an unbeaten 73 from Langton as the last four wickets realised 222 runs. Rapid centuries in reply from Leyland and Ames kept the contest simmering before Wyatt declared on the third day, leaving his bowlers two sessions to force a result. It was not enough and, though Mitchell fell cheaply for once, Wade and Dalton dug in to bat out the draw and earn South Africa a momentous series victory[2]. In the sage words of the journalist R. C. Robertson-Glasgow, England's reverse amounted to 'a rude but helpful shock'. So helpful, in fact, that within three years English batting was back in the rudest of health, electrified by the heady potential of Hutton and Compton.

Some of the press were quick to point out that had the Tests been played over four days instead of three, England would have won or at least drawn the series. The uncomfortable truth was that the fortunes of the national team were at a decidedly low ebb, and had been for a couple of years. Yet, as Dudley Nourse noted, 'We were conscious of the fact that we represented nothing like the threat to the supremacy of English cricket that an Australian side does.' The fact that the Tests had been allotted only three days, he suggested, 'was proof enough that we were not yet considered a Test match force by comparison with Australia'. If South Africa's record in England before 1935 was not of a standard to merit four-day Tests, their triumph at Lord's did much to change that perception, certainly among the public who cheered them as they would their own. England had played Tests of four days' duration in South Africa since the inaugural MCC tour there in 1905–06, but the notion that they required only three days to defeat the Springboks at home no longer held true. However, South Africa would have to wait until 1947 before playing their first four-day Test in England.

After five months on tour Wade's team departed Southampton aboard the *Windsor Castle* on 20 September and docked in the Cape two weeks later, a weary but contented crew. 'We had set out unheralded but returned with something very precious: Test match success,' Nourse wrote. 'There was much still to be done, but at least there seemed a solid enough foundation.' Tragically, that foundation would be shaken to its core by the sudden death of 'Jock' Cameron at the age of 30. The man the victorious Springboks regarded as their rock, a rallying point and talisman, had contracted typhoid fever on the voyage home after putting in at Madeira and died within a month of his return. 'It was an irreparable loss,' Nourse recorded, 'and cricket suffered a mortal blow by his passing.'

Wisden posthumously named him one of their Five Cricketers of the Year for 1936 (alongside Bruce Mitchell) and ranked him second only to Australia's Bert Oldfield as a wicketkeeper, likening his stumping style to the 'nonchalant gesture of a smoker flicking the ash from a cigarette'. There were few more destructive or cleaner strikers of the ball either, and in a game against Yorkshire in 1935 he memorably thundered 30 off an over from the seemingly unassailable Verity.

Louis Duffus, who covered the tour of England for the *Star* in Johannesburg, had good cause to remember the thrill of another Cameron innings: his match-turning 90 in the Lord's Test. He was on the telephone to Johannesburg, dictating his copy for the late Saturday sporting edition while Cameron was still in full swing. 'There is no need for alarm at South Africa's poor score,' he reported. 'The wicket is bad and England will have to fight for runs. Cameron is playing the innings of his life . . .' Just four months later those words would prove especially poignant[3].

The first full tour of South Africa by Australia, therefore, could not have come at a worse time for the Springboks. Australia had made only two brief visits to the Union before, always on the back of tours to England, and on 14 November 1935 they docked in Durban amidst much anticipation. As South Africa were now the conquerors of England, and Australia had successfully reclaimed the Ashes a year earlier, some newspapers saw fit to promote the five-match series (the Tests were scheduled for four days) as a battle for the world championship title. If it was, there was only one side in it, and the Australians – 'as cocky as ever', in the opinion of Duffus – breezed to a 4–0 victory. At least there was no Bradman, who had stayed at home because of ill health, to compound the pain, though as Dudley Nourse put it: 'They might have let us keep our fame for a little while.' Nourse, in fact, was the one bright spot for South Africa, hitting a magnificent 231 at Johannesburg to score over 500 runs for the series: the innocent at Lord's had grown into a fully-fledged Test match batsman.

The reasons for the Springboks' capitulation were no great mystery. The distressing loss of Cameron so soon after their return from England and the rigours of the 'most fatiguing tour any country has undertaken', Duffus concluded, had sapped their last drop of resolve: 'Many of them were patently stale.' The Australian batsman Jack Fingleton may have flogged South Africa's bowlers far and wide during the Tests but he was more than sympathetic to their plight. 'Anybody who has played 54 innings or who bowls six thousand balls in a short English summer has been not on a sporting so much as a business tour,' he reasoned. 'Someday somebody will realise just how damaging it is to the sport and the individual to play cricketers into the ground over a short period.' It is an argument that has echoed loudly down the years.

Before returning to South Africa after the tour of England, Duffus had closed the typewriter case and taken a short excursion through Europe. After five months of punishing deadlines and the daily slog of churning out copy to order, he was jaded and as much in need of a break from the game as the players themselves[4]. He motored through France and Belgium, with no special destination, and on into Germany. In Munich he observed the swastikas and 'the spreading militaristic mood', but paid it little heed: 'It was 1935. We were not thinking of war.' The Rhine, Mosel Valley, Bavaria and Baden-Baden proved the perfect tonic and a welcome rest, before his thoughts turned to cricket once more. 'They were saying "Heil Hitler", but it seemed less important than "how's that?"', he remembered.

Louis George Duffus was South African cricket's constant companion and its foremost writer on the game, though he liked to dabble now and again in tennis, golf, rugby union, athletics and baseball. He reported on the ups and downs, the ebb and flow of his country's fortunes for almost 40 years, never missing a beat or a Test match in that time. In fact he covered 110 in all, making seven tours of duty to England and three each to Australia (the country of his birth) and New Zealand. He also played cricket and baseball for Transvaal and was a good enough wicketkeeper to earn selection for a Test trial but not quite good enough to win a cap. He was a journalist who 'went unashamedly for vivid imagery', *Wisden* declared, 'priding himself as a stylist on no more vain grounds than that he abhorred hackneyed composition'. He was among the fortunate ones, who operated during a period when cricket writers were granted the ultimate luxury of space by their newspaper editors. His route into the profession was hardly conventional, though.

He had been working as a bookkeeper in Johannesburg when, on a whim and a prayer, he decided to hand in his notice and follow H. G. Deane's 1929 South African side to England. His prime motivation, he admitted, extended no further than a burning desire to see the world. So, armed only with a commission to provide fortnightly articles for the Johannesburg *Star* and a cheap return ticket on a Union-Castle steamship, he traded accounts and a steady income for adventure and uncertainty. 'I resolved to leave Highveld, home and ledgers for whatever kind of wicket St. Christopher thought fit to roll out.'

On arrival in England he made his way to Fleet Street and knocked on the doors of its sports editors, offering to supply regular progress reports and advance information on the touring Springboks. His reward, much to his surprise, was to find himself in immediate demand (this was in the days before news agencies regularly gathered such material for the press) and articles by Louis Duffus soon appeared in the *Evening News*, the *Daily Mirror* and the *Daily Mail* carrying the byline, 'The Transvaal wicketkeeper who is covering the tour'. Buoyed by his success, the rookie reporter purchased a baby Austin and set off to follow the Springboks around England – a venture that would turn into a glorious road trip.

'What a life it was,' Duffus wrote, 'rising on summer mornings in quaint countryside hostelries, piling a bag or two into the back of the little open car, bowling up hill and down dale to the next cricket ground.' There were perfect roads, 'with none of the dust or corrugations of the highways of the veld, foolproof signposts and faithful maps, and England in all its fresh loveliness. This was the idyll of the journey'. And there were days when he had to shut himself away, typing into the small hours in order to catch the mail for South Africa, before returning to the road 'with all the greater relish when the tasks were done'. He got to know Neville Cardus along the way, took an icy plunge in the Lake District with Bruce Mitchell, 'slept blissfully under one of England's immaculate haystacks', and rubbed shoulders with the greatest bowler the world had known.

The glowering Sydney Barnes was 56 years old when he opened the bowling for the Minor Counties against the South Africans at Stoke. 'A tall lank figure, he stood erect, grey temples and a hard weather-beaten face autographed with outdoor life,' Duffus recalled. He had retired from Test cricket 15 years earlier, but figures of eight for 41 in the tourists' first innings showed he had lost none of his legendary skill or aura of menace. His fast-medium spin – an art form that has long since disappeared from the game – still spat and sizzled off the surface, just as it had during an epic South African summer in 1913–14.

It was in the last tour before the First World War that Barnes collected a world record 49 wickets in a series, from only four Tests. He would have plundered more but, notoriously hard to handle and disagreeable at the best of times, he refused to play in the fifth at Port Elizabeth after a wrangle over money. Barnes by all accounts was simply unplayable on matting, and a South African side that included Herbie Taylor, the country's first great Test batsman, and the stolid left-hander 'Dave' Nourse (father of Dudley) were routed 4–0. Yet Taylor managed to score 508 runs in the series and, despite being dismissed five times by Barnes, engaged in one of Test cricket's truly titanic duels. The Englishmen were unanimous that nobody had ever attacked Barnes, at his best, with more consistency and panache than the young Springbok.

Taylor played his last great Test innings – 121 – in the fifth Test at The Oval during the 1929 tour; but he was past his prime by this time and had been unable to prevent England from sealing a 2–0 series victory. Described by Duffus as an exuberantly young side the Springboks were far from humbled. Cameron embellished his reputation while Mitchell and Dalton successfully served their apprenticeships, emerging as cricketers who would guide their country's fortunes in the years running up to the Second World War, and beyond in the case of Mitchell. After 39 matches Duffus had sailed to South Africa with the rest of the team – his faithful baby Austin loaded into the hold.

Unemployed now that the tour was over, he ruefully accepted he had no other option than to return to the world of bookkeeping and ledgers. But three days away from Table Bay he received a telegram that would change his life for ever. It was from the sports editor of the Johannesburg *Star*: 'If you care to consider a post with us, I'm sure the company would be glad to make you an offer.'

———

South Africa played their first Test match against England at Port Elizabeth in March 1889, though for those who participated in it the status of Test cricketer was not conferred until some years later. Sussex's C. Aubrey Smith brought with him a cast of amateurs, professionals and adventurers (six had not even played a first-class game before) that was clearly not meant to be representative of English cricket. Nonetheless, they won a low-scoring game convincingly enough by eight wickets inside two days. Smith captured seven for 61 with his medium-pacers before heading to the Hollywood Hills, where he found fame playing a succession of impeccable English gentlemen in movies such as *The Prisoner of Zenda* and *The Lives of a Bengal Lancer*. He was, as *Wisden* quaintly put it, 'The only England captain to star in a film with Elizabeth Taylor (Mervyn LeRoy's *Little Women*).'

Smith's men also brought with them something more tangible: the Currie Cup. Sir Donald Currie, chairman of the Union (later the Union-Castle) Line and the tour's sponsor, donated a trophy for Smith to present to the side who put up the best performance against them. Kimberley were the beneficiaries and it duly became the country's premier domestic trophy.

Seventeen years later an England side flying the colours of MCC arrived in South Africa, led by Pelham Warner. The Boer War had been over for only three years and the tour was seen in some quarters as a fence-mending exercise, though the Springboks visited Britain in 1901 while the war was in progress but played no Tests. However, in keeping with many of the early teams that left for the Cape, Warner's party carried too many passengers and was more significant for the players left behind than those selected. England regularly kept their best players at home in preparation for sterner battles ahead with Australia. Warner, despite appearing to be all things MCC, was not even first choice as captain. Instead Jack Mason, the highly regarded Kent all-rounder, had been approached on 3 July 1905 to lead the side. Mason was revered by the county's professionals, among whom Frank Woolley was not alone in considering him the best captain he had played under. But he was also a full-time solicitor and declined the invitation: perhaps he knew something that Warner didn't, for MCC was comprehensively beaten 4–1, becoming the first England side to lose a Test series in five visits to South Africa.

The Springboks employed four googly specialists – Reggie Schwarz, Aubrey Faulkner, Gordon White and Ernie Vogler – and by the end of the series their mastery over the England batsmen was complete. Bernard Bosanquet, an Englishman, is acknowledged to be the inventor of the art, but it was the South Africans who first cultivated and exploited the effectiveness of wrist-spin on the international stage. Bosanquet taught Schwarz the googly while they were team-mates at Middlesex, and the magic formula was passed down 'like an heirloom', in the words of Duffus, to Faulkner, White, Vogler and Balaskas.

By 1912 South Africa were established as the third Test-playing nation, though they were very much the junior partner, and competed in the star-crossed Triangular Tournament – a world championship in all but name – with England, the hosts, and Australia. The competition was the creation of Abe Bailey, a South African diamond tycoon, but suffered from one of the wettest summers on record. Although the Springboks had defeated MCC 3–2 in 1909–10 fielding their four-pronged leg-spin attack, the sodden wickets negated their bowlers and befuddled their batsmen to the extent that they lost all but one of their six games in the tournament. The final was won by the hosts, who beat Australia by 244 runs at The Oval on the fourth day of the inaugural timeless Test to be staged in England.

In 1922 MCC returned to South Africa to contest the first series between the countries after the First World War, bridging a gap of eight years since Sydney Barnes had been in fearsome, full flow. It was agonisingly close and the tourists finally prevailed in a timeless decider at Durban, winning by 109 runs after the Essex professional 'Jack' Russell became the first man to score a century in each innings of an England–South Africa Test match. The game lasted six days and was the first to be played to a finish on South African soil. Bizarrely, the start of one day's play had to be delayed while groundstaff removed handfuls of frogs from the coconut matting.

The changeover from matting to turf was well under way when Percy Chapman's MCC party visited at the start of the 1930s. For the first time, a Test match in South Africa was played on a grass pitch, at Newlands in Cape Town; another two were played in Durban. But England had the rug pulled from under them in the opening Test in Johannesburg when

'Buster' Nupen produced figures of 11 for 150 to bowl the Springboks to the only victory of the series, by 28 runs. The Norwegian-born Nupen bowled fast-medium and spun the ball like a top on the mat, with what Duffus described as 'a delightful flowing action, pace off the pitch and a sharp break-back which he combined with a periodical slight turn from the leg'. Uniquely, perhaps, Nupen was as innocuous on turf as he was majestic on matting.

Hammond, on his second tour of South Africa, batted beautifully, scoring 517 runs for the series, and in the second Test at Newlands he not only opened the batting and the bowling but later kept wicket after George Duckworth tore a ligament in his hand. The tourists could have done with the likes of Harold Larwood, 'Gubby' Allen, Douglas Jardine, Hobbs, Woolley and Sutcliffe, all of whom were either unavailable or had been left at home. In the end their attempts to get back into the series were thwarted by a combination of rain and the fighting qualities of the Springboks, who at Newlands passed 500 for the first time in a Test against England; on turf, too.

———

South Africa had closed the gap, and for the next two years during an interval between 1932 and 1934, when there were no tours at home or abroad, their cricketers bedded in and worked hard to sharpen their skills on turf pitches. Duffus considered it at the time to be 'probably the most important [period] in the history of the game in the Union'. The transition from matting to turf was designed to make South Africa more competitive abroad (though Australia would remain their nemesis for some years to come) and, in the English summer of 1935, perhaps sooner than anyone might have expected, 'the harvest was reaped'. The fact that South Africa turned out so many proficient first-class players during those years, 'having little more than weekend cricket', was a constant source of wonder, as the England fast bowler Ken Farnes explained: 'When they have touring teams out there even the Currie Cup languishes, and Test teams have to be selected on known form, club matches, and actual performances against the touring team. As in Australia, there is no professional cricket.'

Now, for the first time in a series in South Africa, a full-strength England side would play all five Test matches on turf pitches, over four days' duration and with eight-ball overs, too. In addition, it was agreed that the fifth Test would be timeless if the rubber was level or one side was leading 1–0. Hammond had never made a secret of his dislike for matting wickets, and before the 1938–39 MCC party sailed from Southampton for the Cape, he told reporters, 'We have a good, young team and shall soon be playing on the fine pitches of South Africa. When last I was there they played on matting, now it is turf, and I believe very fine turf.' The selection of Hammond's team was seen in South Africa as testament to the progress made by its cricketers and, turf or matting, many expected the Springboks to crown their series victories over England in 1930–31 and 1935 with a third successive triumph. As *Wisden*, somewhat portentously, put it, 'Our cricketers know full well that England has not beaten South Africa in a Test since 1929 and that upon them rests the responsibility of restoring the cricket prestige of the country where the game was cradled.'

The nucleus of the victorious 1935 South Africa side – Mitchell, Nourse, Dalton, Langton, Balaskas, Viljoen and Eric Rowan – was still in place and, though Cameron's loss remained keenly felt, it would be partly offset by the addition to the ranks of Alan Melville. In fact, Melville bypassed the ranks altogether and was appointed captain of South Africa for the 1938–39 series, despite never having played in a Test. The series was something of a homecoming for the tall, right-handed batsman after spending the past five years in England.

He had established a reputation as an exquisite timer of the ball and a ruthless destroyer of fast bowling, first for Oxford University and then at Sussex, where he led the county for two seasons. Remarkably, before his arrival in England, he had never played on turf wickets before, but introduced himself by scoring 78 against Kent and taking 118 off Yorkshire at The Parks. During that time he put his studies ahead of Test cricket and resisted overtures from Douglas Jardine and others to switch allegiance to England, before returning to South Africa in 1936 to take a job with the Johannesburg Stock Exchange. As an arch-stylist he gave Hammond a run for his money, even his defensive strokes were 'worth blueprinting', the journalist Denzil Batchelor enthused. Jackie McGlew, the former South African captain, described Melville as 'a gentleman to his fingertips: sleek, suave and sophisticated. His shirtsleeves were buttoned at the wrist, there were razor-sharp creases in his cream flannels and, more often than not, a sparkling white cravat knotted inside his collar'. A brilliant fielder, who moved with equal facility between silly mid-on, mid-off or slip, he would almost certainly have walked into an England XI had he wished.

By general consensus, Melville inherited a Springbok side that lacked a top quality wicketkeeper-batsman

(Cameron had left a huge void to fill), an opening attack worthy of the name, and a left-arm spinner. They would have to wait until the timeless Test in Durban before discovering a wicketkeeper to match those qualifications. But the form of Transvaal's uncapped Norman Gordon – the 27-year-old had been the outstanding performer in the 1937–38 Currie Cup with a crop of 39 wickets – suggested that, if they didn't know it yet, they already possessed a pace bowler of genuine Test-match class.

Three
The Call of Africa

*'We used to look hastily at the newspapers every
morning to see whether the Luftwaffe had bombed
our homes' – Norman Yardley*

The lavender hull and clean white lines of a Union-
Castle steamship were easily identifiable to the crowd
on the quayside when, at 8 a.m. on 4 November 1938,
the *Athlone Castle* tied up in the shadow of Table
Mountain. Equally as distinguishable, and interspersed
among the throng on the main deck, were the dark
blue, red and yellow MCC blazers of the 12th team
from England to tour South Africa. For the 13
cricketers who were making their first visit to the
Union (only the West Countrymen Hammond and
Tom Goddard were not seeing it through new eyes) it

was a spectacular entrance into the Cape, and all attention was fixed on the towering wall of mountain, swathed in its tablecloth of cloud. 'It was a wonderful sight,' Len Hutton remembered. 'Table Mountain dominated everything, and Cape Town looked like a toy town beneath it.' Eddie Paynter even wondered whether the landmark had not been 'deliberately decorated for the occasion'. He was just as impressed by the gleaming line of luxury limousines, waiting on the quay to whisk them straight to their hotel.

Louis Duffus, now the correspondent for the *Natal Daily News* in Durban, was among the first of the pressmen and autograph hunters who went aboard to meet the players. Hutton was the most sought after and managed to throw the autograph hunters off the scent by sitting quietly behind a newspaper – a ploy that was easily rumbled by the members of the South African press. He was immediately surrounded and, in his quiet and understated manner, politely referred all requests for interviews to the manager. Hammond, having just breakfasted, looked the picture of unruffled calm and urbanity amidst the commotion and sudden surge of activity that accompanied a vessel's arrival in port. 'We had a very nice trip and we are all looking forward to our cricket,' he informed reporters in a perfunctory exchange. Personally, he explained, he was keen to catch up with old friends again. This was his fourth trip to Cape Town, a city that would always command a special place in his affections. Twelve years earlier he had taken a coaching post in the suburb of Green Point and been dazzled by the beaches and startlingly modern buildings that 'New York would be proud of'. There must have been a satisfying symmetry to the fact that he was returning to one of his favourite cities as the captain of England.

The manager Jack Holmes was eagerly into his stride, emphasising the point that he had brought with him 'the best side England can produce at the moment', but saw no reason why South Africa should not have as good a team. Holmes, who had assumed the captaincy of Sussex from his good friend Alan Melville in 1936, added that everyone was well prepared for the tour, having taken advantage of the swimming pool and gymnasium during the voyage. The sun-worshippers among them already sported tans.

Life on board one of 'the most powerful British motorships afloat', as the Union-Castle Line advertised its fleet, had clearly agreed with the players. Ever since James Lillywhite's pioneers set the precedent in 1876, England touring teams always travelled first-class and the nine professionals in Hammond's party basked in the same luxuries and comforts as the amateurs. There were fancy-dress nights, dances, music and deck games – golf, tennis, quoits – in which the Yorkshire amateur Paul Gibb proved a dab hand, winning four of the ship's competitions to relieve Hammond of his crown. Two weeks at sea, with a short stopover in the Mediterranean sun of Madeira, was an infinitely more pleasurable experience for a cricketer than the 6,000-mile, two-month passage to Australia when most days were an inevitable battle against boredom and oppressive heat. As Hammond, who sailed on the *Orion* with 'Gubby' Allen's MCC side for the 1936–37 Ashes series, commented at the time: 'She was a lovely ship, but I wish she – well – had wings.' The only concerns aboard the *Athlone Castle* had been the injuries sustained by Norman Yardley and Len Wilkinson, and the regular boat drill – a pervasive reminder of the looming threat of war.

Yardley suffered a cracked rib and a deep cut under his right eye after slipping and falling against a rail while running on deck (they had encountered rough seas between Southampton and the Bay of Biscay). The cut required several stitches and, after being confined to his cabin for a couple of days, he had to stay hidden behind a pair of dark glasses for the rest of the voyage. 'Somehow, a silly rumour got back to England that there had been trouble in the team and that I had been involved in a scrap,' he recalled. It was

Wilkinson's injury that turned out to be the more puzzling, though. He had complained of pain in his left hand during the voyage and it was only after the side's arrival in Cape Town that an X-ray revealed a fracture to a knuckle. He could provide no logical explanation for it, and any connection between Yardley's cut eye and Wilkinson's broken knuckle was vigorously dismissed by the management.

After the usual tedious (for the players) round of functions and various speeches – Hammond's addresses were notable only for their brevity – the team was anxious to get down to business. Yardley and Wilkinson were both missing against a Western Province Country District XI in the opening fixture, only four days and two net sessions after their arrival. Hammond and Paynter struck rapid centuries and MCC scored 589 in a day to win by an innings and 342 runs. The game was little value other than a gentle warm-up, acclimatising players to the light and the conditions against a side that was no more than club standard; but Hammond and Paynter ensured that the batsmen set a scorching tempo to the tour and Verity and Goddard, extracting turn and bounce, ran through the Country XI in quick succession on the second day.

The batsmen did not let up and further victories quickly followed against Western Province, Griqualand

West and Orange Free State. Kimberley, in Griqualand West, is the diamond capital of South Africa and the pitch there, they discovered to their astonishment, was even polished like one. In fact, it was almost black, and closer inspection by the players revealed that it contained not a single blade of grass; Farnes likened the surface to 'an arterial road'. The batsmen feared the worst but were more than a little relieved when it turned out be one of the most placid they played on, racking up a first-innings total of 676 in a shade over six hours. Hutton, Edrich, Paynter and a restored Yardley filled their boots with centuries and Verity picked up another handful of wickets, 11 in all.

During their stay in Kimberley the players visited the offices of De Beers and saw the Big Hole, a relic of the diamond rush of the 1870s. All that remained from those feverish days was a disused man-made crater, measuring a full 17 hectares (42 acres) in circumference. The three scratch golfers in the team, Hammond, Ames and Valentine, had some fun driving golf balls into its vast interior, where they were swallowed up by the deep green water some 800 metres below. By the time they claimed their fifth success from six games, against North-Eastern Transvaal in Pretoria – the most northerly point of their travels – the batsmen had already notched 12 centuries between them on the continent's perfect pitches. Paynter, with three, was at the front of the queue in iridescent form, followed by Hammond, Hutton and Yardley with two, and Edrich, Valentine and Bartlett on one each.

Only Natal at this point had managed to restrict them to a draw. There had been rain before the start of play in Durban and Hammond was mocked by a spectator when he walked out to inspect the wicket carrying his umbrella. 'Where's your bowler hat and spats?' he was asked. The Englishmen, in turn, were amused by the sight of oxen pulling the mower in the outfield and by the regular bursts of music that played over the public address system during the intervals. Some of the music was a bit old-fashioned, in the view of William Pollock of the *Daily Express*, who dryly recalled that the idea had been tried in England on a couple of occasions, only to be hastily dropped: 'Perhaps some of the spectators complained that it disturbed their sleep.'

The tourists had the better of the draw once the rain cleared and, in reply to Natal's 307, Hutton and Hammond completed their second centuries in another batting exhibition; Edrich, with 98, just missed out on his after putting on 207 for the opening wicket with Hutton. No doubt the England captain felt he had a point to make, for he was in sublime touch during his 122 and his cover-drives raced over the baize, striking the fence with a satisfying thump. Even Nourse admitted that there was a certain pleasure to be had fielding to a Hammond hundred: 'He always delights when making runs. Perhaps the bowlers don't take the same view, but as a fielder I loved watching those strokes, powerful and secure through the covers and the turn to leg off the body.'

It was an impressive start to the tour, Duffus reported, and 'the public flocked to watch the matches in unprecedented numbers'. It was almost, he added, 'as if they sensed that the days of watching first-class cricket were limited – though few in this blessed country could have seriously entertained thoughts of war'.

For Duffus, who spent four months accompanying the tourists on their journey, it was the most glorious of times: 'It was my sixth cricket tour – the third round South Africa. Repetition dulled none of its attraction. There is no end to the fascination of big cricket, nor the romance that ever spreads itself over the vivid canvas of South Africa. I doubt whether there is a land where cricket is played that provides more glamour, more colour.' The players were in huge demand, and on one occasion kept the train waiting at a wayside station while they were greeted by a local cricket club. After being hustled off to a specially convened function, Hammond and

Holmes took the precaution of inviting the driver and guard along, so that the train could not continue its journey without them. By the end of their travels, Duffus calculated, they had covered some 12,000 miles on the articulated Garratt steam locomotives of the South African and Rhodesian railways. It was almost 900 miles from Johannesburg to Cape Town alone, and 1,000 between Durban and Cape Town, and included in both cases at least two nights on the rails.

These black armour-clad giants of the veld were the pride of a nation and the most powerful trains in the southern hemisphere. They did not lack for opulence, either: a plush observation car was attached for the convenience of the players on all journeys. The introduction of air-conditioning to most South African trains by the end of thirties also added materially to their comforts. In the company of his fellow scribbler Pollock, Duffus got to know each individual well, even if the broad Lancashire accents of Paynter and Wilkinson frequently left him baffled. A tour of South Africa did not yet have the status of an Ashes adventure and, for the England players who toured Australia in 1936–37 in the company of Fleet Street's finest and what seemed like half the Australian press corps in tow, the presence of so few journalists made for a welcome relief.

An England team invariably gathers together the most diverse personalities and temperaments in the game, and the 1938–39 party, Duffus soon discovered, was no exception:

> 'Art thee oop, Doog? Art thee oop?' Down hotel passages at dawn, shouted above the rhythm of wheels as trains clattered their morning way over the veld, rose the sounds of Eddie Paynter's dialect, calling Doug Wright. From bathrooms sometimes came the lusty unmusical strains of 'Bye Bye Blackbird'. A university accent on your left and the rich brogue of Yorkshire on your right – the social ends of England gathered in a place like distant Bulawayo ordering breakfast because, if they shared no other characteristic, they had a common love of cricket: 'I say, waitah, two eggs, turned . . . Steward, cold lom . . .'

They were also a tightly knit, high-spirited group who, thrown together for four months, indulged in harmless pranks on each other and 'forgot for a while that at home they might walk to the wicket through separate gates and never appear at the same social function'. In fact, their companionship and inexhaustible sense of fun owed much to the influence of Hammond and Holmes. On the voyage out, the England captain and manager devised a series of stunts and amusements to keep the team up to the mark, or at 'concert pitch' as Edrich called it. The players entered into it wholeheartedly. Every Monday at breakfast each man had to wear a bow-tie – the more extravagant the better – or pay a forfeit of five shillings. There were no exemptions. Fines were ruthlessly doled out to any slackers and the proceeds handed over to a charity. On appointed days in the week a penalty of sixpence was imposed on anyone who failed to drink with his left hand. Team members also carried a bottle top with them at all times and could be challenged at any moment – even in mid-innings – to produce it. 'No wonder it was a joyous tour,' Duffus wrote. Paynter was in no doubt that the captain's 'experience of both amateur and professional status' had much to do with it.

Yet privately Hammond worried about injuries, or more pertinently an injury befalling either Verity or Farnes. The batting, he knew, would take care of itself but a lack of depth in the bowling (he had decided to use himself only sparingly) placed a heavy onus on the fitness of his principal spinner and fast bowler. Both had taken wickets in the early tour matches, notably Verity, whom Hammond regarded as 'infallible', the left-armer slotting automatically into that irresistible rhythm of his. Farnes had bowled with genuine pace when the wickets allowed (seven for 38 against Western Province at Newlands), and though Edrich might occasionally match him for speed in short spells he could not, in the view of his captain, 'keep on the spot for very long'. As South Africa's strength lay predominantly in batting, the prolonged fitness of both men was imperative. So Hammond was aghast when, just days before the start of the first Test, Verity walked into the lobby of the team hotel in Pretoria with his shirt and hands covered in blood.

Verity and Wright, in fact, had been taking a stroll in the city when they stumbled across a street fight. One of the men had been stabbed and, after the assailants ran off, the cricketers flagged down a taxi, lifted the victim inside and saw him safely to hospital. Hammond had been barely able to contain his relief. 'I thought he [Verity] had had a street accident,' he explained, 'and nearly jumped out of my skin at the thought that England's safest bowling hands might be permanently damaged.' The incident did not end there.

The team's visit to Pretoria preceded by a week the centenary celebrations of Dingaan's Day, or the Day of the Covenant as it is also known, when the Voortrekkers' victory over the Zulus at the Battle of Blood River on 16 December 1838 is commemorated. It is an event ingrained in Boer history. The celebrations, Farnes recalled, were not entirely devoid of anti-British feeling, 'and large numbers of Dutch youths had grown beards to make them look like the forefathers they were honouring'. Pollock detected that the atmosphere in the city was 'tricky and electric' and, like any good newspaper man, filed a piece on Verity and Wright for the *Daily Express*, only to have it, in his words, 'sub-editorially sensationalised'. The story read as though the pair had been involved in a street brawl, rather than acting as the good Samaritans they were. 'I wasn't very popular with Walter Hammond and Jack Holmes over that,' he remembered.

Hammond, nonetheless, decided to take all precautions and Verity was rested for the seventh game of the tour, against a powerful Transvaal at the Wanderers in Johannesburg, where the first Test would be played a week later. The tourists had yet to concede a century but immediately found themselves up against Bruce Mitchell on a plumb wicket after South Africa's new captain Melville won the toss. The bowlers would have needed no reminder of Mitchell's qualities as a relentless accumulator of runs, but they got one anyway as he mixed stern defence with controlled strokeplay in a chanceless 133. Another Test batsman, Ken Viljoen, almost completed a second before Wilkinson, the pick of the attack, wheeled a top-spinner through his defence, allowing Melville to declare at 428 for eight at lunch on the second day.

The crowd had barely settled into their seats after the interval when Eric Davies, pitching short, struck Hutton on the head with the third ball of MCC's reply. Hutton was not only knocked out but the ball rolled from his head onto the stumps, and he was carried from the field and rushed to hospital. A tall, athletic right-arm quick bowler who made his Test debut against Australia in 1936, Davies could be distinctly slippery for a few overs – Farnes reckoned he was 'the original fast merchant' – but lacked accuracy and stamina. Hutton confessed that he simply lost sight of the ball: 'Les Ames told me that he did not see his first ball either. Fortunately it passed by his head six to eight inches away[1].'

For the first time the tourists' batting faltered. The sight of the stricken Hutton crumpling slowly to the turf appeared to have unsettled a few minds, and Edrich, Paynter, Hammond and Yardley were soon retracing their steps to the pavilion. Hammond's dismissal, aiming a back-foot drive to a lifting delivery from the lively Norman Gordon, was more the result of 'Chud' Langton's stunning reflexes in the gully. The ball travelled so fast that the force of it spun the fielder around and he ended up with his back to the wicket in completing the catch. Only an assured 109 from the unflappable Ames saved MCC from further embarrassment. The hallmarks of any century by

Ames – the speed and fluency with which he scored his runs, the nimble footwork and booming straight-drives – were much in evidence. He had batted for 145 minutes when he was undone by a rapid inswinger from Davies, who wrapped up the tail on the third day to finish with six for 82 out of a total of 268.

Melville, however, declined to enforce the follow-on, opting instead for batting practice, and the game drifted towards an inevitable draw. During an afternoon session punctuated by showers, Davies learned that he had been recalled by South Africa for the first Test, starting on Christmas Eve. He would be joined by his fellow pace bowler Gordon and the Western Province opening batsman Pieter van der Bijl, an Oxford blue and former amateur heavyweight boxer, who were among five new caps named by the selectors. The solid and familiar core of the side was provided by Mitchell, Nourse, Langton, Viljoen and Dalton.

Hutton's name was missing from the England XI after Hammond judged that it would be 'unwise and unfair' to pick him. His place at the top of the order went to his fellow Yorkshireman Gibb, who was one of three Test debutants alongside Yardley and Wilkinson. Gibb's experience of opening the batting for his county tipped the vote in his favour, though he was short of runs and confidence having managed a highest score of 28 from only three innings on tour[2]. There had been no such problems for Yardley and Wilkinson, who were in the full flush of form. Wilkinson's zip and accuracy against Transvaal had impressed Hammond, and he would form a triumvirate of spinners with Verity and Goddard. Wright was the odd man out on this occasion. The success of Australia's spinners during the 1935–36 Test series in South Africa, when the ball turned prodigiously on the turf and Clarrie Grimmett filled his swag bag with 44 wickets, had not been lost on the England selectors. Hammond believed it was an area where his side held an advantage, too, and Wilkinson could expect to be busy on his debut.

Instead, it was Gibb who exceeded all expectations in a Test that acted as a barometer for the batting excesses to come[3]. England amassed 713 runs in their two innings, setting a record aggregate for matches between the two countries at that point; in all a total of 1,211 runs were scored during the four days. 'The first thing we discovered when the Tests began was that the wickets were either over-prepared or else were unnaturally fine,' Hammond wrote. 'They were batsmen's wickets all the time, and it is no reflection on the fine batting performances of our men to say so.' Indeed, Hutton's absence was barely felt. To Paynter went the distinction of scoring a century in each innings, while the bespectacled Gibb hit 93 and 106, amply rewarding his captain's faith in him; the pair also shared in second-wicket partnerships of 184 and 168.

Gibb had seized his opportunity, making the most of a reprieve early in the first innings after cutting Langton hard towards Melville in the gully. The captain could only parry the ball into the slips, where Van der Bijl juggled with the rebound but failed to cling on. Yet, as Gibb was expected to be no more than a stopgap until Hutton's return, his success presented Hammond with a dilemma: what to do with Edrich? The all-rounder's failure in both innings (he was dismissed by the fourth ball of the match from Davies and contributed a scratchy 10 in the second) was the continuation of a run of low scores that had plagued him since the series with Australia in 1938. By his own admission he was struggling: 'As soon as I saw a Test crowd my bat felt loose in my hands, and whether I attempted stonewall defence or tried to force the pace, all that happened was my wickets rattled down. I just could not get going.'

Edrich cut a doleful figure in Johannesburg set against the exuberance of Paynter. The diminutive Lancashire left-hander may have been no more than 5 foot 4 inches but he batted with a tall man's stride; not for him any suggestions that he was too small to play Test cricket. A hearty puller and cutter – 'me fancy cuts', as he liked to refer to them – Paynter delighted the huge holiday crowds with his sense of adventure and belligerence. During the first-innings alliance with Gibb the spectators left neither man in any confusion as to which they preferred to watch. Pollock was even moved to wonder whether Gibb 'with very few strokes in his bat was not one of the worst-best batsmen I have ever seen'. *Wisden*, too, was inclined to damn him with faint praise: 'It would have needed a shrewd critic to discern, when watching him play a long innings, that he was more than a determined and solid university and county batsman.' Gibb's idiosyncrasies, though, endeared him to all his team-mates, whether it was befriending dogs, eating vast quantities of ice-cream (he was reputed once to have consumed 22 at a sitting) or finishing all the fruit on the table after every meal. He was also, unsurprisingly, the butt of many a prank.

The British Pathé newsreel of the first Test offers a rare and fleeting glimpse of Gibb and Paynter batting together. At just on a minute it is all too short, but shows Gibb with shirt sleeves rolled high, driving into the covers for runs and studiously shouldering arms to a ball outside off stump. He usually batted in a headband, or a tennis eyeshade, to prevent sweat from dropping onto his glasses. Paynter, in a cap, scores through the on side with two perfectly timed strokes off his pads and is off scampering down the wicket as soon as the ball leaves his bat. Johannesburg was often described as a miniature New York and most of the action is filmed side-on, against a backdrop of skyscrapers that are so close they almost appear to be encroaching on the pitch. 'Even the cars on the wide streets are of American design,' Paynter noted. There is an elegant glance off his hip by Hammond for a single, while Ames executes a robust pull to the boundary off Davies, whose bowling is characterised by a long gallop to the stumps and an unusual follow-through that sends him veering in the direction of cover-point at the last moment, like a train coming off the tracks.

The footage concludes with a shot of the Christmas Eve crowd filing out of the ground at the close of the first day, leaving a sea of bottles, glass and strewn newspaper in their wake. Pollock reported that play was accompanied by regular announcements reminding spectators not to throw glass onto the adjoining greyhound track, where the almost space-age tote dwarfed the scoreboard.

———

A crowd of 22,000 – a record for a Test in South Africa – was in place on the Boxing Day resumption to see England bowled out for 422 and Valentine fall three short of his century[4]. Batting, however, was not so straightforward for the Springboks. Van der Bijl and Melville failed to resist the wiles of Verity, and the captain was snaffled for a duck in his first Test innings. Contrasting half-centuries from Mitchell and Nourse appeared to have averted the danger, before Goddard deceived Nourse in the flight, triggering a late clatter of wickets. The off-spinner had the nightwatchman Gordon stumped off the next ball and completed a memorable hat-trick by dismissing Billy Wade, the wicketkeeper, with one that turned sharply and unexpectedly.

For E. W. Swanton, a freelance journalist commentating for the BBC at the time, it was the equivalent of cricketing gold dust. Swanton, with half-an-hour's slot to fill each evening, was pioneering the first live broadcast of an overseas Test match to be relayed to England, where the year was fading in a flurry of snow and freezing temperatures. As Cardus put it: 'Cricket girdles the earth nowadays.' Desperate to make an impression, Swanton was running out of patience, if not words, to describe the monotonous run-gathering and Mitchell's stonewalling. 'As I sweated in my tiny enclosed box I imagined English listeners by the thousand falling asleep over the Yule log,' he recalled. Then Goddard struck. In the next few moments Swanton's future, and that of ball-by-ball broadcasting, were simultaneously assured. 'So Tom was on a hat-trick. Here was a situation the drama of which even this tyro at the mike couldn't miss. Wade came slowly in, went nervously through the business of taking guard, looked around – and was promptly bowled. Only five Englishmen in Test history had done the hat-trick before Tom Goddard. It was quite a story[5].'

Yet, despite Goddard's timely intervention, South Africa finished only 32 shy of England's total after the leg-spinning all-rounder Eric Dalton hit 102, staging a bold recovery in the company of Viljoen and Langton, who struck an unbeaten 64, batting at No. 10. The talented Dalton can have rarely played a more invaluable innings for his country. He scored his runs with an unusually heavy bat and even the snicks flashed like lightning to the boundary in the rarefied air. Hammond declared England's second innings on 291 for four, setting the Springboks a target of 324 to win in just under three hours. It was never a realistic proposition and Mitchell, occupying the crease for the entire 165 minutes for his 48, dead-batted the game into submission.

Ironically, the most lucrative Test to be played in South Africa at that stage terminated in barracking – much of it aimed at Mitchell – and criticism of

Hammond's tactics. The local press accused the England captain of sacrificing the game to allow Gibb to complete a Test century on debut, the eighth Englishman to do so. The opener had spent several anxious minutes becalmed on 98, before reaching his landmark in just under three hours. After Gibb's dismissal Hammond made every effort to speed up the scoreboard, often advancing down the track to the quicker bowlers and swatting the ball to the boundary with what Pollock likened to tennis shots. 'It was a disappointing end to a good match, but Hammond must take the blame for killing the game,' one journalist wrote. 'Despite this, Gibb's feat is remarkable in Test cricket, but the point is whether the game is worth more than an individual performance.'

Hammond had shuffled his bowlers like a card sharp when South Africa batted again, but Mitchell would not be moved and walked off at the end with the jeers of the home crowd ringing in his ears. Pollock rarely wasted an opportunity to inject some colour into proceedings and remarked of Mitchell: 'No wonder that while some people swear by him, others swear at him.' He added, in much the same vein: 'Someone asked me, when the game had gone to sleep for a time, if I thought that four days was long enough for a Test match. I said there were occasions when I

Walter Hammond (centre) shakes hands with the mayor of Southampton before sailing for the Cape, watched by Pelham Warner (left), chairman of the selectors. Behind them (l–r) Doug Wright, Reg Perks, Ken Farnes and Hedley Verity form a quartet of bowlers.

The 1938–39 MCC party in South Africa. *Back, l–r:* Bill Edrich, Doug Wright, Eddie Paynter, Bill Ferguson (scorer). *Middle:* Len Wilkinson, Hedley Verity, Hugh Bartlett, Tom Goddard, Reg Perks, Len Hutton, Paul Gibb. *Front:* C. R. Ridgway (South African manager), Ken Farnes, Norman Yardley, Walter Hammond (captain), Les Ames, Bryan Valentine, Jack Holmes (manager).

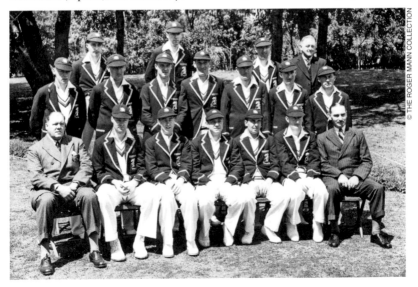

Above: The Western Province Country District XI take the field for the opening game of the tour at the Strand, Cape Town, where MCC won by an innings and 342 runs.

Yorkshire's Len Hutton (left) and Paul Gibb open the England innings on the first day of the second Test at Newlands. Hutton missed the first Test at the Wanderers after being knocked unconscious by a bouncer from Transvaal's Eric Davies days earlier.

Alan Melville leads out the South Africans at Newlands, followed down the pavilion steps by the vice-captain, Bruce Mitchell.

England regularly drew huge crowds, and 10,000 packed the ground to capacity for the second day's play at Newlands on 2 January 1939.

The spiky Eric Rowan struck an unbeaten 89 in South Africa's second innings at Newlands. The journalist Louis Duffus wrote that his success was founded on '70 per cent cocksureness and 30 per cent ability'.

Newlands, one of cricket's wonders of the world, in all its splendour during the tea interval on day three.

Kent's Bryan Valentine was one of three England centurions in the second Test. A carefree batsman, *Wisden* recorded that his 112 contained so many strokes 'it almost amounted to recklessness'.

Above: Reg Perks (left), Bryan Valentine and Eddie Paynter soak up the sun on one of South Africa's many dazzling beaches.

Left: Hedley Verity, the left-arm spinner and fulcrum of England's bowling attack, photographed in 1938.

Below: Alan Melville's Springboks walk out for the start of the third Test at Kingsmead, after Walter Hammond won the toss on the seventh successive occasion as England captain.

Norman Gordon appeals successfully for leg-before against Len Hutton (31); Paul Gibb, in the headband, is the batsman at the other end.

Eddie Paynter dispatches a ball from Eric Dalton to the boundary on his way to a commanding 243 at Kingsmead. Hammond, who shared in a stand of 242 for the third wicket with him, watches approvingly.

Above: England prized the wicket of Bruce Mitchell above all South Africans. He was his country's top run-scorer during the series with 466, including a magnificent 109 in the third Test.

On the mighty Zambezi above Victoria Falls. *l–r:* Bill Ferguson, MCC scorer, C. R. Ridgway, South African manager, Louis Duffus, cricket correspondent for the *Natal Daily News*, and Hedley Verity (leaning forward); Eddie Paynter and Doug Wright are closest to the camera.

© THE ROGER MANN COLLECTION

High jinks on the golf course. Among the England players are Walter Hammond (first left), Bryan Valentine and Les Ames (third and fourth left); Hutton is behind Ames, and Paul Gibb is first from the right, next to E. W. Swanton, who was covering the tour for the BBC.

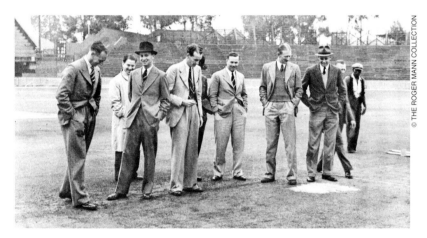

© THE ROGER MANN COLLECTION

© POPPERFOTO/GETTY

Above: Pitch inspection during the rain-ravaged fourth Test at the Wanderers. *l–r*: Hedley Verity, Bruce Mitchell, Alan Melville, Eric Dalton, 'Chud' Langton and 'Bob' Newson.

The versatile Langton produced the best figures by a pace bowler in the series: five for 58 to dismiss England for 215 on the opening day of the fourth Test.

The South African team for the timeless Test in Durban. *Back, l–r:* E. A. Deavin (manager), Eric Rowan, 'Chud' Langton, Pieter van der Bijl, 'Bob' Newson, Ronnie Grieveson, Norman Gordon. *Front:* Ken Viljoen, Bruce Mitchell (vice-captain), Alan Melville (captain), Eric Dalton, Dudley Nourse.

Left: Ronnie Grieveson formed a potent alliance with Eric Dalton (below), twice stumping Hammond off the all-rounder's leg-breaks during the timeless Test. His 75 in South Africa's first innings was the highest score by a wicket-keeper in a debut Test innings at that point.

Below: Natal's Dalton contributed a sparkling half-century and six wickets.

Reg Perks excelled on his Test debut at Kingsmead, returning figures of five for 100 from 41 overs in South Africa's first innings, often matching Ken Farnes for speed.

The dapper Ken Viljoen not only made two visits to the barber's during the timeless Test; he also stroked an elegant 74 in South Africa's second innings.

Bill Edrich ended one of Test cricket's most fraught baptisms when he hit 219 – an innings partly fuelled by champagne – after England chased 696 for victory at Kingsmead.

Below: Edrich edges Norman Gordon through the slips during his marathon knock.

Opening batsman Pieter van der Bijl goes on the attack against England's tiring bowlers. He missed out by three runs on becoming the first South African to score two centuries in a Test.

Doug Wright's leg-breaks proved expensive at Kingsmead, but his ability to conjure the occasional shock delivery served England well.

Below: The muscular Dudley Nourse deserted his attacking principles during the timeless Test, reaching a painstaking century in six hours and four minutes.

Below: Les Ames's work behind the stumps at Kingsmead was a triumph of sustained focus and skill, taking two catches and conceding only six byes.

Above: 'Bob' Newson of Transvaal was South Africa's most economical bowler in Durban, delivering 68.6 overs at a cost of 149 runs.

Eddie Paynter, all 5 foot 4 inches of him, batted with a tall man's stride and was England's leading run-scorer in the series, hitting 653 at 81.62.

Below: The immaculate Hedley Verity bowled 766 balls (95.6 overs) in the timeless Test, capturing four wickets for 184 runs and rarely strayed from a good length.

© POPPERFOTO/GETTY

© CENTRAL PRESS/STRINGER/GETTY

TOTAL
654
FOR 5 WICKETS

BOWLER
1 0

BOWLER
6

No 6
BATSMAN
0 4

LAST PLAYER
140

No 5
BATSMAN
1 7̄

LAST WICKET
FELL 6̄ 5 0

S.AFRICA 1 0 1 1   ENGLAND 3 1 6

Above: Frozen for all time, the amazing Kingsmead scoreboard after the final curtain. The two not out batsmen were Ames (17) and Valentine (4); the last man dismissed was Hammond for 140.

Ken Farnes (left) and Hedley Verity (right) are greeted by Farnes's father at Waterloo Station on MCC's return from South Africa.

Above: Worcestershire's Reg Perks proudly shows off an assegai while his wife looks on.

Walter Hammond (left) appears to have an animated conversation with a member of the public after the team's arrival at Waterloo Station from Southampton.

Norman Gordon took instantly to Test cricket, establishing himself as the leading wicket-taker in the series with 20, pipping Hedley Verity by one.

Below: He was also the first Test cricketer to reach a century in years and celebrates the landmark with help from Mike Procter (right) and Fanie de Villiers on 6 August 2011.

thought it was too long.' The newspapers agreed that both sides would need to raise the tempo considerably if the second Test at Newlands was not to go the same way.

England: 422 (Paynter 117, Valentine 97, Gibb 93; Gordon 5-103) & **291-4 declared** (Gibb 106, Paynter 100, Hammond 58); **South Africa: 390** (Dalton 102, Mitchell 73, Nourse 73, Langton 64no, Viljoen 50; Verity 4-61, Goddard 3-54) & **108-1**. Match drawn.

England would at least have Hutton back to form a new opening partnership with Gibb at Newlands. Edrich retained his place, despite his lack of runs, and Yardley dropped out of the XI. For South Africa, Dalton and Viljoen were unavailable and Balaskas and Rowan, two architects of the 1935 conquest of Lord's, were recalled. There was only a three-day turnaround before the start of the second Test on New Year's Eve; so, shortly after the conclusion at the Wanderers, both teams boarded a train and headed south on the 900-mile journey to Cape Town. The long trek passed through the Great Karoo, an arid, desolate place of soaring temperatures, made more bearable by the soothing tones of Valentine's gramophone. The Kent amateur never travelled without it, rarely missing an opportunity, as Duffus put it, 'to remind us of revue and glamorous nights at Drury Lane'.

During the trip the players briefly stretched their legs at De Aar junction, where the desert heat easily nudged 90°F and beyond in the sun. 'The Karoo looked a merciless region from our hot carriages,' Farnes observed. 'But at sunset the land became much more friendly, and cool purple shadows gave a quiet blessing to the earth after the brazen torture of the day.' In his 1940 autobiography, *Tours and Tests*, Farnes revealed a fascinating glimpse of the writer he aspired to be, often creating the impression that he was on a restless quest for greater fulfilment. He had been working on a novel on tour but appeared to have lost confidence in it, abandoning it halfway through. He also sketched, scribbled some poetry, and found the time to attend an art exhibition and a classical concert, along with a couple of nightclub jaunts in the company of the irrepressible Valentine. A young housemaster at Worksop College in Nottinghamshire, Farnes was eloquent and deep-thinking and, unlike the majority of his contemporaries, did not require the services of a ghost writer. On his return to England he was commissioned to write several articles for *Boy's Own Paper*, from whose pages he could so easily have stepped.

He had struggled badly in the high altitude of Johannesburg, however, finishing with one for 104 from 30 overs. 'After chasing the ball the fielders found they had no breath left, and I found that after bowling only a few balls I was completely blown,' he admitted. 'I came to dread playing there, for the eight-ball over was gruelling.' One glance at the Newlands wicket after their arrival in Cape Town was enough to confirm his worst fears: it was another batsman's paradise. Mercifully, for his bowlers, Hammond won the toss for the sixth successive time in a Test, and England reached 131 for two on a rain-interrupted day.

New Year celebrations were muted by normal standards and the players' thoughts naturally turned to home, where Chamberlain had assured the British people that 1939 would be 'a more tranquil year than 1938'. The cricketers kept a constant eye on events in Europe, Duffus reported; they were always frantic for the latest newspapers and often discussed Hitler's speeches. As young men who would be called up to fight in the likelihood of another war, they were unpersuaded by what Yardley referred to as 'the frightful soothing of statesmen', and most had already made up their minds that conflict was inevitable.

Verity, in fact, had been convinced as early as 1937 that war was coming and predicted it would last for six years. According to Hutton, he prepared himself by spending much of his leisure time on tour meticulously studying a small arsenal of military manuals and training pamphlets he had brought with him. Farnes, on a more introspective bent, had concluded that, 'God isn't interested in man's affairs in the slightest and Hitler's disturbances won't be altered by any amount of prayer.' Such fears and doubts, Yardley remembered, steeped their days: 'There was something unreal about that winter away from home. We used to look hastily at the newspapers first thing every morning to see whether the Luftwaffe had bombed our homes, and everyone wondered whether we could get one or two more seasons of cricket before we had to take up something more deadly.'

———

On the pitch, 1939 carried on where the old year left off and runs continued to pour from the bat, as though someone had left the tap on. There were centuries from Hammond – on his favourite ground – and Ames and Valentine, when play restarted on 2 January in front of another capacity holiday crowd. The captain's 181 was undoubtedly one of his finest, an exhibition of great freedom and power, before he declared at 559 for nine early on the third day. Valentine's roistering 112 contained so many strokes that, according to *Wisden*, it 'almost amounted to recklessness'. Nobody suffered more at their hands than the little 'Greek chemist' Balaskas, whose figures of 24-0-115-0 would be his last in Test cricket. The alchemy had evaporated.

There were further rumblings in the South African press at the timing of Hammond's declaration, and many believed that Melville's side had no other option but to play for a draw. Mitchell clearly thought so, but proceeded to take the situation to absurd lengths, spending almost four hours at the crease for 42. Once again there was no pace in the wicket for Farnes but Verity, at his scheming best, picked up five for 70 and, despite a muscular 120 from Nourse, Hammond was able to enforce the follow-on. Farnes provided some early hope for England by removing Mitchell cheaply, but South Africa's batsmen successfully closed out the game – Van der Bijl and Rowan making 87 and 89 respectively – to ensure that they travelled to Durban for the third Test all square. It was a drab ending, Farnes recalled, relieved only by the changing hues of Table Mountain as it towered over the ground, and the applause of a drunken sailor from a tree: '"Well played, Viljoen!" he cried again and again. "Good ol' Viljoen!" Actually, Viljoen was a thousand miles off in

Johannesburg – he had been unable to get leave to play in the match.'

England: 559-9 declared (Hammond 181, Ames 115, Valentine 112, Gibb 58; Gordon 5-157); **South Africa: 286** (Nourse 120; Verity 5-70) & **201-2** (Van der Bijl 87, Rowan 89no). Match drawn.

———

The tourists moved on to Port Elizabeth, where Hutton hit 202 against Eastern Province and the slumbering giant that was Farnes rediscovered his appetite for wickets, building up a rare head of steam on a pitch of extreme pace. More significantly he carried his form into the third Test in Durban, starting on 20 January. This time the toss proved a profitable one for Hammond to win, and England amassed 469 for four declared in a little over six hours. Paynter stroked a scintillating 243 (334 minutes and 24 fours) to exceed 1,000 runs for the tour, and Hammond an effortless 120, his 20th Test century. Hammond also got his declaration in early for once on a wicket that was mostly easy-paced, allowing his bowlers two days and two sessions to win the game. Moreover, there was just enough grass on the surface to keep them interested.

Fittingly, in what he considered the most English of South African cities (with its clean streets, good buildings and interest in the arts), Farnes produced his best bowling performance of the series. He captured four for 29 to rout the Springboks for 103 and, sensibly used by Hammond in short bursts, snatched three more after they followed on, 366 behind. Not surprisingly, Mitchell provided the main obstacle to England's progress, batting 190 minutes for 109 – he even dusted off some handsome cover-drives among his 14 boundaries – before edging a lifting delivery from Farnes to Ames. Bowling to a cordon of slips and encircling close fielders, Farnes unsettled all the South Africans with his pace and accuracy, and put the seal on victory by an innings and 13 runs, claiming the last wicket with a day to spare. Verity, as ever, provided invaluable support with three for 71 from 35 overs.

Wisden recorded that the light deteriorated badly during the latter stages of the Springboks' innings though, curiously, none of the batsmen thought to appeal against it. Inevitably Paynter and Farnes shared the headlines but, as Nourse wrote, the result was nothing short of a personal triumph for Hammond: 'From the moment almost when he won the toss he had the match won for his side. Besides a spirited and flawless century, he switched his bowlers magically. He held magnificent slip catches [five in all] and took a wicket as a bowler just to prove himself the "General" complete.'

England: 469-4 declared (Paynter 243, Hammond 120); **South Africa: 103** (Farnes 4-29) & **353** (Mitchell 109, Rowan 67, Viljoen 61; Farnes 3-80, Verity 3-71). England won by an innings and 13 runs.

———

It was also in Durban that Gibb became involved in one of the more bizarre incidents to befall an England cricketer on tour. Yardley explained that a few of the team had managed to acquire some 'incredibly good but ancient cars for knockabout use' during their stay in the city. The thought of England's cricketers careering around the streets of Durban in these ancient vehicles boggles the mind, and demonstrates the level of autonomy granted to players on tour in those days. Gibb had paid a sum of about £5 to become the proud possessor of what he vigorously maintained was an original Ford. But no sooner had he parted with the money and driven off downhill than the car started to spit fire and smoke. He had not gone far when the hill grew steeper, and it was at this juncture, he discovered to his horror, that when he put his foot hard on the brake nothing happened, except the car went faster and faster. Unable to control it, Gibb ended up ploughing through the middle of a fruit stall, where he came to an ignominious and somewhat sticky halt. As luck would have it there was an equally amusing postscript to this misadventure.

The next morning, having settled up with the indignant stall owner, Gibb somehow managed to humour his vintage Ford through the traffic to Kingsmead, leaving it parked at the ground out of harm's way before the start of the game. But on reaching the pavilion he was apprehended by a policeman who informed him that, as the car was neither licensed nor insured, he would have to report immediately to a police station. 'As Paul was everlastingly getting pranks played on him, he simply laughed at the policeman's momentous gravity, supposing that one of us had given the man a couple of shillings to play a joke on him,' Yardley related. 'The more Paul laughed the more portentous the officer became, and the more unable the rest of us were to do anything but hold our sides.' The matter was eventually resolved, though not without the cost of much embarrassment to Gibb, particularly after it found its way into a newspaper under the headline, 'Test cricketer in car crash'[6].

After the Test victory at Durban the tourists decamped to Rhodesia for a two-week interlude, where they spent a couple of days at Victoria Falls and took a trip along the mighty Zambezi. Farnes was particularly entranced and felt that he had entered 'the Africa of my imagination for the first and only time on the tour'. There was some cricket, too, at Bulawayo and Salisbury, against a Rhodesia XI, with both matches played on matting; the country had yet to graduate to turf pitches. The experience would leave an indelible impression on the team. At Bulawayo the bare outfield had to be covered in white sand to enable it to dry after a rainstorm and, according to Farnes, 'made you feel as if you were playing in snow'. At Salisbury the outfield at least had some grass on it but the game was again badly hampered by rain; so to dry the thick clay that formed the base of the matting wicket, the groundstaff simply doused it in petrol and set it ablaze. After several minutes of leaping flames and thick black smoke, the fixture went ahead as scheduled.

It was still raining when they returned to Johannesburg for the start of the fourth Test on 18 February. A victory for England at the Wanderers would wrap up the series 2–0 and eliminate the need for the fifth Test in Durban to be played to a finish. However, a draw or even a win for South Africa would ensure a timeless decider. In the end the fourth Test was spoiled by the weather (the third day was a washout) and gave the inescapable impression that everything was building slowly towards a timeless conclusion. England spent what little of the match there was on the back foot, despite Hammond calling correctly at the toss for the eighth successive Test. He had appeared in two minds whether to bat or bowl in the damp conditions, and Duffus reported that he hesitated for an uncomfortably long time before opting to bat[7].

The wicket offered regular assistance to all the bowlers and not a single century was scored. Hutton, with 92 in England's first-innings total of 215, came closer than anybody before Mitchell bowled him with a ball that spun wickedly. The most potent threat came from Langton, who exploited the conditions so artfully that he produced the best figures by a pace bowler in the series, five for 58 from 19 overs. In a quest for quick runs Melville pushed himself to the top of the order, with Mitchell moving to No. 4 to play the sheet-anchor role, and went on the attack. The switch instantly paid off. The captain hit 67 in an opening partnership of 108 with Van der Bijl at more than a run a minute and declared on 349 for eight, leaving England four hours to save the match.

They duly did so, reaching 203 for four, but not without an anxious moment or two. Indeed, had

Hammond been caught early in his innings off the impressive Gordon, things might have been interesting. Ronnie Grieveson, who gave a highly competent display behind the stumps on his debut, did well to get his glove to a difficult leg-side chance but could not hold onto it. As it was, Duffus wrote, 'Hammond, having survived, won back his mastery and, in the closing stages, gave a brilliant exhibition of footwork, placing and timing' to finish unbeaten on 61. And with that, all eyes turned to Durban for the timeless Test.

England: 215 (Hutton 92; Langton 5-58) & **203-4** (Hammond 61no; Gordon 3-58); **South Africa: 349-8 declared** (Rowan 85, Melville 67, Mitchell 63). Match drawn.

Four

A Threepenny Opera

'The South Africans have got this timeless Test all wrong. Evidently they think that the big idea is to stay in as long as you like and score as slowly as you can' – William Pollock

Day one: Friday, 3 March

One of the South Africans could not bring himself to watch and retreated to the dressing-room where, according to Nourse, 'he sat, with fingers crossed, hoping to be of assistance to Melville'. The other nine players leaned forward intently over the balcony rail, refusing to take their eyes off the two captains as they made their way out to the middle; most had their fingers crossed, too. The willowy 6 foot 2 inch Melville, some three inches taller than the square-shouldered, thick-set Hammond, drew a threepenny bit from his blazer pocket and showed it to the England captain, before spinning it high into the warm Durban air. After losing four tosses on the bounce to Hammond, Melville had decided to swap his usual half crown for an ordinary threepenny bit, given to him several days earlier by Norman Gordon. The coin, however, came with an assurance.

Gordon, in fact, had won it off Hutton during the interminable train journey from Johannesburg to Cape Town after the first Test, when the teams travelled together and the pair wiled away the idle hours by playing cards. The Englishman lost half a crown and, being short of change, settled his losses by throwing in a threepenny bit, or a 'tickey', as it was known in South Africa. Gordon hung onto the twelve-sided piece and, according to Louis Duffus, handed it to Melville a few days before the timeless Test in Durban, eager for some of his luck to rub off on the captain. 'If you toss with this you can't possibly lose,' he told him.

On the pavilion balcony the South Africans watched the coin land. 'Melville bent down anxiously to scan it,' Nourse recalled, 'and rose with a smile. Hammond lifted his head and then bowed as Melville said something to him, and we knew in that moment that we had won the first round at least.' In losing the toss for the first time in nine Tests since becoming England captain, Hammond admitted he had been momentarily distracted by the sight of the new coin and changed his call to tails at the last second. There was a thumbs-up from Melville to the players' balcony, 'and jubilantly we went into the dressing-room to tell our team-mate that his crossed fingers had done the trick,' Nourse added. Seconds later a huge cheer from around the ground set the timeless Test in motion. The whimper would come later.

All week the talk had been of the timeless Test, and interest in the match was reported to have reached 'unprecedented proportions'; many of the big hotels in Durban were booked out. The anticipation had been heightened by South Africa's forthright display in the fourth Test – much of which was credited to the positive influence of Melville and the apparent loss of form by several England players. The tourists, as Farnes pointed out, had given their most ragged performance of the series in Johannesburg: 'We had prayed for rain and a sticky wicket to bowl on. Now that we had it our bowlers, Hedley Verity and Tom Goddard, who usually account for sides for ridiculously small scores on such wickets, bowled worse than they had ever done in such conditions, and had no luck either.'

Suddenly, the Springboks' chances of squaring the rubber were being talked up by the newspapers and embellished in offices, trains and bars across the country. The confidence of the South African selectors was reflected in an unchanged side, announced on the final day of the fourth Test almost two weeks earlier. Grieveson's sparky presence behind the stumps in Johannesburg appeared to have had a galvanising effect, while 'Bob' Newson, having replaced the tearaway Davies as opening bowler, proved an effective and accurate addition to the attack. The batting had a reassuring ring about it, its depth accentuated by the presence of the ever-dangerous Langton at No. 9.

Inevitably, injury and tiredness were catching up with England, and Hammond had no choice but to tinker with his selection: out went Wilkinson and Goddard (the former on fitness grounds, the latter on lack of form) and in came the mercurial Kent leg-spinner Doug Wright and Reg Perks, the Worcestershire pace bowler, for his first cap. 'Some of the England players, particularly the bowlers, are showing signs of staleness. I think the whole team has probably passed its peak,' Pollock informed the readers of the *Daily Express*.

Paynter, who had pulled a thigh muscle, was only passed fit on the morning of the match after undergoing a strenuous run around the ground. Once again Hammond had been reluctant to omit Edrich, and the all-rounder retained his place in the XI, leaving

Yardley and Bartlett surplus to requirements. The pair could have been forgiven for feeling hard done by. Certainly Bartlett's attacking credo might have been put to more imaginative use by Hammond, and there appeared nothing to lose in awarding him a first cap. Disappointingly, he was the only member of the party not to appear in a Test during the series.

Edrich's 150 against Natal at Pietermaritzburg in the only game before Durban had undoubtedly saved his place – that and his usefulness as a bowler. Made in enervating heat, many were calling it his finest display of the tour, leading MCC to their ninth victory. 'Although I say it, I did not give a chance in that innings and wondered whether, at this late stage, form was not coming back, after all,' he said. 'But that was the trouble – I could not be sure.' In 11 Test innings since making his debut against Australia at Trent Bridge in 1938 Edrich had managed only 88 runs, with a highest score of 28, and knew better than anyone that this was effectively his last roll of the dice.

Having achieved their first objective of winning the toss, the Springboks' tactics, in theory, were simple: to bat as long as possible and to amass as many runs as they could before the wicket started to break up, which in the natural order of things it was bound to do. The mechanics of timeless cricket invariably enable the side that wins the toss to establish supremacy through sheer weight of runs, when the over-prepared wicket is at its best, and then drive home their advantage with the ball on a wearing surface against opponents dog-tired and psychologically demoralised after several fruitless days in the field. As Hammond, who was certainly no apologist for timeless Tests, put it: 'The idea is to tire the bowlers with a huge score, and then go on and make it bigger still.' Much, in fact, as England had done to Australia at The Oval seven months earlier, though on that occasion the mishap to Bradman was not part of the original script.

Few expected the wicket, or indeed the match, at Kingsmead to last beyond five days. As the tourists' itinerary had allowed for one last fixture – the 19th – against Western Province, starting on 11 March in Cape Town (they would sail for home six days later), there appeared to be ample time for the completion of both games. Nourse had no doubts. 'Quite obviously the winning of the toss at Kingsmead was of paramount importance,' he said. 'Remember, the match was being played in Durban where the weather even in March cannot be relied upon. I had decided that whoever won it would win the match within the week.'

Gordon's 'lucky coin' had done the trick.

———

A blustery sea breeze was blowing almost diagonally across the pitch, noisily rustling the palms and casuarina trees, when Farnes prepared to bowl the first ball of the timeless Test in bright sunshine. Barely 4,000 spectators were in the ground to watch the opening overs, though the numbers would expand steadily throughout the day. The Kingsmead wicket, brown in appearance, with little or no grass, was in marked contrast to the one that had offered the bowlers a rare ray of hope during England's victory there in the third Test in January. The only encouragement was the breeze, providing the possibility of some swing at least for the quicker bowlers, and perhaps a trace of early moisture in the surface, but no more. It was typical of the many over-prepared, artificial pitches that England had encountered on tour – 'one to gladden groundsmen's hearts,' as Pollock put it, 'never mind about bowler's hearts.'

The cricket writer Ralph Barker described Kingsmead as 'an open ground with no tall stands to spoil the light', and as such it was equally advantageous to players and spectators alike. It was a pleasant ground and made a welcome change from Johannesburg's vertiginous skyscrapers and steep stands which, according to Farnes, made it sometimes difficult for players to see the ball. Kingsmead's single wooden stand and pavilion were on one side of the ground, side-on to the wicket, and the low terracing that encircled the square 'did not interrupt the view of flat, rather featureless country from the pavilion balconies'. To the right, Barker continued, 'lay the fringes of the city of Durban, while to the left the field rose into mounds on which were planted trees to commemorate the scoring of a century in a Test match on this ground'. Hammond and Paynter had already planted saplings there in the third match of the series. But such was the number of batsmen who perpetuated the tradition during the timeless Test that it might have warranted a small plantation of its own.

Farnes, bowling off 11 paces in what was described as 'a canter rather than a gallop' (his run-up was considered short even by the standards of the time), started with eight dot-balls to the equally imposing Van der Bijl. Surrounded by three short-legs and an array of slips the 6 foot 4 inch opener bent so low in the crease, Pollock observed, that 'his body was almost at right angles to his bat'[1]. At the other end Perks, bowling to Melville, swung the ball in against the breeze at a brisk pace. Runs came ominously slowly.

Melville was content to pick up the occasional single and, aside from a confident appeal by Ames for a catch behind off Perks early in his innings, appeared his usual sedate self, batting stylishly but within himself. Van der Bijl, though, was intent only on survival and it would take him 45 agonising minutes to get off the mark, at which point Melville had moved his score to 19. 'Mostly, Van der Bijl just stopped the ball with a bat so dead that it had hardly strength to trickle as far as the close-set fielders,' Pollock wrote. Six runs were scored in the first 25 minutes and Edrich, one of the close fielders, claimed that the pair started so passively it was 'as if they had eternity before them'.

It was left to Farnes to fire the opening salvo of the timeless Test. Pounding the ball in at just short of a length on leg stump, and using his height and brute strength to detonate lift and life from the wicket – no mean feat in itself – he repeatedly peppered Van der Bijl about the body. The sturdy Perks quickly followed his example and he was soon commanding as much respect as Farnes in terms of pace. During this period barely a ball went by without leather striking flesh or the batsman taking evasive action before the missile smacked with a satisfying thud into Ames's gloves – the wicketkeeper and slips positioned almost equidistant to the stumps and the boundary. Melville did not escape the barrage, and was doubled up by a ball from Farnes that struck him in the chest after he missed with an attempted pull. But it was Van der Bijl who bore the brunt. 'Once, he left the field to stuff more padding into his trousers,' Duffus wrote, 'and on his return was immediately hit on the same place.' Pollock even wondered if it was not his own fault: 'He takes guard on the leg stump, and as the ball comes up, moves across to the off stump, leaving the bowlers no stumps in view.'

It was a torrid passage of play and a vivid re-enactment of the 1932 Varsity match, when Farnes subjected Van der Bijl to a similar ordeal by fire. On that occasion, Swanton recalled, the Oxford boxing blue 'was not nearly nimble enough on his feet to avoid a man of Farnes's pace "digging them in", and I can hear now the bull-like bellows that echoed round Lord's as he took the ball on various portions of his anatomy'. Seven years later Van der Bijl appeared no more nimble on his feet but, acutely aware of his limitations, often allowed the ball to strike him on the body, thereby eliminating the risk of deflecting it to the close fielders or edging a catch behind. What he lacked in technique and dexterity he more than made up for in courage and concentration. Paynter commented later that Van der Bijl was hit several times just below the heart by Farnes. In the words of one South African player, he took his blows uncomplainingly, 'risking personal injury rather than his wicket'; though as Duffus, who was unable to resist the boxing analogy, admitted, he was struck so frequently it made for painful watching:

> He designed his innings as he might a heavyweight title fight. In the first round – early in the morning – he was forced into a corner and took untold punishment. He became the fast bowlers' punching bag. As Farnes and Perks attempted to wrest kick from the wicket by dropping the ball short, he was smitten hip and thigh without flinching. He played with a blind, stubborn courage. Time and time again it seemed possible for him to avoid injury without endangering his wicket, but he took blow after blow on the body, and the bowlers played on his weakness.

For Hutton and Edrich, crouching in their short-leg positions, it might have revived memories of Farnes's bowling in the Gentlemen's versus Players match, on another docile wicket, at Lord's eight months earlier. Both men recorded that it was the quickest they faced in their careers. Edrich was struck on the head via his glove by a ball that flew viciously from short of a length. 'The ball jumped like lightning straight at my eyes. I tried to play back, a defensive stroke, while turning my head and lifting my hands.' When he came to, it was to be told he had been caught in the gully. Farnes was smarting after being dropped by England following one of his notoriously erratic performances in the second Test against Australia at Lord's and, according to Edrich, he had been 'like a tiger at feeding time'. Hutton managed a half-century that day but believed they were runs as hard-earned as any he scored, before he too fell to Farnes: 'I felt I was at the wrong end of a shooting gallery. He pitched just short of a length and had the pace and height to make the ball rear spitefully and alarmingly at head height. I find it impossible to think bodyline could have been more frightening and intimidating.'

That Farnes was England's strongman was not in doubt – whether it was flogging life out of a dead pitch, or lifting a two hundredweight gold brick with one hand on a visit to the West Rand Consolidated mine in Johannesburg (to the astonishment of his team-mates). 'I had heard a rumour that if you could pick up one of these bricks with one hand you would be considered entitled to have it,' Farnes remembered. 'I managed to do so, but waited in vain for the authorities to say, "Right! It's yours!"'[2] A fitness fanatic, Farnes obviously prided himself on his strength and physical appearance. According to his biographer, David Thurlow, he had taken a Mr Universe-style bodybuilding course earlier in his career and was not averse (usually after some gentle coaxing) to showing off his stomach muscles in the dressing-room. There had also been a brief fling with shot putting during his days at Cambridge, and he once threw an impressive personal best of just over 42 feet.

Somehow Van der Bijl and Melville survived the onslaught to take South Africa safely through to lunch, despite managing only 49 runs in 105 minutes. Even the Farnes storm temporarily blew itself out and, when Hammond summoned him back into the attack for a short burst just before the interval against the breeze, he was noticeably down on pace. Melville cut him for two and then drove him elegantly through the covers for three. It was the nearest the Springboks came to a boundary all morning.

Van der Bijl resumed his innings after the interval having padded his body with towels for protection, but his travails continued when a snorter of a ball from Perks cracked him on the elbow. Pollock reported that the blow 'caused him to holler'; Duffus that 'he held his arm out stiffly and sank to his knees', staying there for several anxious moments before the pain subsided. Farnes, well rested after lunch, persisted in testing out the middle of the wicket and again the opener was pummelled about the body. The umpires, if they deemed it necessary, could have intervened at this point. The rules in 1939 stated that a bowler could be warned or removed from the attack for 'the persistent and systematic use of fast short-pitched bowling'. Perhaps they didn't feel Farnes had strayed beyond the bounds of legality, or perhaps they concluded that much of Van der Bijl's troubles were self-inflicted.

Nourse, watching from his ringside seat on the players' balcony, recounted that on at least one occasion he heard the batsman call to the bowler, 'Cut it out, Ken', but added, 'Farnes would just grin at him and deliver another in the same spot.' Described by Nourse as 'a soul of patience and forbearance', it was as close as Van der Bijl came to raising a protest during his innings, and even then he made it almost apologetically.

Despite this, runs came more freely and 24 were added in half an hour after lunch on the 'slow-motion scoreboard'. Finally, Melville produced the first shot in anger – 135 minutes since the start of play – latching on to a no-ball from Perks and pulling it handsomely to the fine-leg fence. The long wait was over, and Melville followed it by completing his half-century in 152 minutes of fierce concentration; Van der Bijl was not even halfway to his. The captain celebrated with a flourish of boundaries off Wright, Verity and Hammond (who continued to under-bowl himself), before posting the century stand with an on-drive to the ropes off Verity, who was at his most parsimonious having earlier bowled a spell of nine overs for eight runs.

When England did get the sniff of a chance, after a midwicket mix-up between Melville and Van der Bijl, Paynter – normally the most reliable of fieldsman, with a slingshot throw – shied wildly at the stumps from the covers and the opportunity went begging. As if to rub it in Van der Bijl played his first telling stroke in more than three hours at the wicket, straight-driving Verity for four, a shot that was greeted with a roar from the burgeoning crowd. Hammond instantly beckoned Farnes back into the attack, only for Van der Bijl to guide his nemesis to the rails with the most delicate of strokes.

Just when Hammond was starting to wonder where the first wicket might come from, Wright surprised Melville with a ball of extra pace. It was an unlucky end for the captain, though the bowler undoubtedly played his part in it. Wright operated off a springy 15-yard approach to the wicket, involving several hops, skips and jumps (he took a longer run than Farnes) and, with his high, windmilling action, was appreciably faster than other leg-spinners. The Australian journalist and author Ray Robinson memorably described his run-up as looking like 'a cross between a barn dance and a delivery stride'; while *Wisden* noted that even his stock ball had a rare fizz to it. Melville was forced back onto his stumps by a delivery that nipped onto him quicker than he expected and, in attempting to pull it to the boundary, dislodged the bails with one of his pad straps. He was given out hit wicket, having made 78 out of 131 in 200 minutes with five fours.

Nonetheless, it was the start the Springboks had craved and their highest opening stand of the series. 'There was no undue hurry about runs. There was all the time we wanted available and the longer we stayed there the sooner the wicket would begin to wear,' Nourse explained. 'These were the obvious tactics to employ and it would make England's task all the more difficult.'

Melville's dismissal brought Eric Rowan to the wicket, a chirpy, garrulous cricketer who liked to keep up a running conversation with the fielders. Jack Fingleton remembered him as a batsman who would talk to anyone within earshot 'on the particular merits and demerits of the ball bowled, the stroke played, the good or bad fortunes of affairs, the health of the in-fieldsmen's families and so on'. Duffus, while recognising that Rowan could be a remarkable batsman on his day, also described him as 'sometimes exasperating' and believed his success was founded on '70 per cent cocksureness and 30 per cent technique'. His presence appeared to have a liberating effect on Van der Bijl, however. For, no sooner had he arrived at the wicket, than the opener brought up his 50 in 210 minutes with a driven four off Wright. He then proceeded to slip spectacularly out of character by hitting five boundaries off the bowler's next seven deliveries.

A little later he transformed again, this time depositing a ball from Wright on to the roof of the grandstand, with what Pollock described as 'the power of a giant'. But he soon reverted to type, struggling through the 90s, when he might have been dismissed on any of three occasions, before finally reaching his century in four hours and 47 minutes with a deflection to leg off Farnes. Some of the spectators, Duffus wrote, threw their hats into the air in tribute and promptly lost them on the breeze. Van der Bijl had offered only one clear-cut chance, on 70, Wright failing to hold on to a stinging drive off his own bowling.

'For the purposes of timeless Test cricket, it was a valuable innings,' Pollock reported. 'But except during two or three patches, when he seemed to think he had earned a little fun, it was burdensome.' Duffus debated whether a South African Test century had ever been scored 'with such a contrasting mixture of defiance and defence, or consummated in such physical discomfort', and praised him for his staunch endurance. 'It was an innings of painstaking defence enriched by vividly contrasting passages of attack.'

The second-wicket pair had contributed 88 in as many minutes when the unflagging Perks captured his first Test wicket, pinning Rowan in front of his stumps with a full-length ball for 33. The Transvaaler had played his part in wearing down the bowlers, and the sight of Mitchell walking out to join Van der Bijl would have done little to improve the confidence of the fielding side. But only a further ten runs were added before bad light ended play ten minutes early, with the score at 229 for two. Van der Bijl, battered and bruised after batting for almost five and a half hours, was on 105, and South Africa had reached base camp on the long climb to a mountain of runs.

South Africa: 229-2 (Van der Bijl 105no, Melville 78).

Day two: Saturday, 4 March

There was no change in the Springboks' tactics the following morning on another hot, breezy day as they continued their ascent – except that the runs came at an even slower rate. In an unusual move by Hammond, Farnes opened proceedings by bowling to Van der Bijl with only one fielder, Hutton, in front of the batting crease. The ploy was for Farnes to bowl just wide of off stump in the hope that Van der Bijl would be tempted to drive him through the vacant spaces and, in so doing, edge a catch behind. But the opener refused to bite and took the obligatory battering in the process. England did not have to wait long for the first wicket of the day, though. Wright's ability to conjure the shock delivery paid off for the second time in the match when he bowled Mitchell for 11 with a ball that flicked his pad. But even the new man in, the brawny, hard-hitting Nourse, was content to suppress his naturally attacking instincts for the cause, and for a while the runs dried up completely.

With little for the spectators to cheer, there was at least some amusement to be had in the running battle between Farnes and Van der Bijl. At one point, after taking a particularly painful blow on the body, Van der Bijl consulted with Hammond and briefly left the field. When he returned, Duffus reported, 'he appeared much stouter, his waist having been thickened with extra padding'. As there was only a limited form of protection for a batsman at that time – his pads and gloves were often pitifully inadequate against a bowler of Farnes's extreme pace – and certainly no chest or thigh guard, Van der Bijl had done the next best thing and improvised. But with his very next ball Farnes unerringly struck him on an unprotected part of his leg, causing yet another hold up. The crowd instantly saw the funny side, and the spectacle of the batsman limping and hobbling helplessly about the crease, rubbing his injured leg, was greeted with much mirth and a few choice comments from around the ground.

South Africa proceeded to crawl to lunch, adding only 42 runs to the total, seven fewer than they had managed in the opening session on day one. Pollock, as he so often did, had an expression for it: 'Cricket with creeping paralysis.' Increasingly exasperated, he would cable his newspaper later that evening: 'The South Africans have got this timeless Test all wrong. Evidently they think that the big idea is to stay in as long as you can and score as slowly as you like. They have not thought enough about it. The thing is to get as many runs as possible, preferably as soon as possible. Runs count, not how long the team has batted.'

Things livened up briefly in the afternoon. Verity had been making the ball dip in the breeze but it was Perks, 'bowling with plenty of fire', who ended Van der Bijl's marathon vigil with a delivery that swung in late to defeat the bat and clip the top of the stumps. 'At long last,' Pollock wrote. Van der Bijl had occupied the crease for all of seven hours and eight minutes for his 125, an innings that included a six and 11 fours. 'In spite of his slow play the 11,000 crowd recognised the valuable role he had played and gave him prolonged applause as he returned to the pavilion,' Duffus noted. After the addition of only four runs, Perks struck again, locating the edge of Ken Viljoen's bat for Ames to complete a routine catch behind the stumps, reducing South Africa to 278 for five.

However, England's attempts to make further inroads foundered on the broad blade of Nourse, first in partnership with Dalton – who scored a typically belligerent 57 before becoming Farnes's only victim of the innings – and then Grieveson. In what was his first Test innings the flame-haired wicketkeeper showed himself to be a more than capable batsman, equally at home against pace or spin. For the second day running play was curtailed by bad light and South Africa went into the rest day on 423 for six, with Nourse 77 and Grieveson 26, their seventh-wicket stand already worth 55. Pollock calculated that the Springboks were some 200 runs behind where they should have been at this stage in the game, and singled out Nourse for his slow batting. 'One of South Africa's best stroke players has been pottering and poking about for more than four hours for 77,' he despaired.

South Africa: 423-6 (Van der Bijl 125, Melville 78, Nourse 77no).

If the Springboks were wearing the broader smiles on the first Sunday of the match, it was not only because of their commanding position in the game. Each man received £5 expenses (worth about £300 today) for each day of the Test, including rest days – an amount that the *Daily Express* described as 'not a bad reward at all'. Although it was not anticipated at this stage that the match would extend much beyond Thursday or Friday, the South African amateurs could still expect to be some £40 richer by the end of next week. The weather appeared to be playing into their hands, too.

Day three: Monday, 6 March
It rained heavily on Sunday night, and the conditions were dull and overcast when play got under way again in a light drizzle. Miraculously the pitch was unblemished, as Pollock and Duffus discovered after making their daily inspection of the middle. 'Overnight rain did no harm to the pitch at all. It ironed out kindly, and looked so good, with the bowlers' footholds filled in, that it might never have been played upon,' Pollock remarked. The key to this particular piece of alchemy had been the application of a special ruling that empowered groundsmen in South Africa, Australia and New Zealand to roll a pitch before the start of play any time after rain. The Kingsmead groundsman Vic Robins, by using the heavy roller at dawn, had erased any imperfections and effectively

created a new wicket. 'Good for at least another four days,' Duffus concluded.

The threatening weather had an effect on the South African batsmen at least, particularly Nourse who was soon batting with greater purpose, pulling a short ball from Wright vigorously to the boundary to move into the 90s. There was not a scintilla of lift or turn to be had for the bowlers and, amidst the first signs that the mood of the game was changing, the impeccable Verity found himself operating to Nourse without a slip. The seventh-wicket pair raised the 100-partnership in 144 minutes and shortly after Nourse completed his second century of the series – the slowest by a South African – having batted for six hours and four minutes, and struck only six boundaries.

Once again it was Perks who came to England's aid when, with the score on 475 for six, he forced Nourse to drag an attempted pull into his stumps after making 103. It was an innings entirely out of character – he would never bat so painstakingly again in his career – but one, he maintained, that was completely in character with the demands of the game and of putting the Springboks into a winning position: 'The only joy in its execution was the knowledge that I was getting my own back on the bowlers, particularly Verity, and that it would better serve the cause of our bowlers when their turn came. An obstinate delight in holding out their bowlers and keeping them in the field made the slow progress more palatable than it might otherwise have been. The spectators bore the snail's pace with stoic calm.'

Incredibly enough, the young Dudley Nourse had to learn his cricket 'off his own bat' and without any assistance from his famous father. Between 1902 and 1924 'Dave' Nourse was the batting rock on which South Africa's Test game was cast, and the call of duty kept him away from home for much of that time; he was touring with the Springboks in Australia when Dudley was born on 12 November 1910. He was reputed to have given his son just one piece of advice when it came to the art of batting: 'I learnt to play the game with a paling off a fence. Now you go and do the same.'

Dudley Nourse did as he was told and became the acknowledged 'king of street cricket', a young batsman who cultivated his craft in the thoroughfares and parks of Durban, rather than in the nets. Essentially self-taught, his batting style was often described as rough-hewn, but one that was not without the 'occasional glitter of polish', in the words of the journalist Denzil Batchelor. Duffus referred to it as the 'rough wrought metal' of his cricket. More incredibly, his father never saw him play until he was 22, by which time he had established himself in the Natal XI and was only two years away from embarking on his first tour of England, with Herbert Wade's victorious team of 1935[3].

Grieveson, in the company of Langton, pressed on confidently after Nourse's dismissal, completing his half-century and taking South Africa past 500 with a well-timed boundary off Verity through midwicket. Astonishingly, it was the first conceded by the Yorkshireman since the afternoon session of the opening day. Grieveson had reached an accomplished 75 when he gifted Perks a fifth wicket by edging a long hop into his stumps, attempting to collect his fourth boundary. 'Few international cricketers of this country won distinction so quickly,' Duffus wrote of the 29-year-old wicketkeeper. 'There were no frills to his batting, but there was a pervading sense of quality.'

Verity claimed the last two wickets just before three o'clock, wrapping up the innings for 530 after 13 hours' batting, though not before South Africa had registered their highest Test score and Langton had driven him high over the sightscreen for six, with what Duffus described as a 'wild whoop'. Perks earned the noble figures of five for 100 from 41 energetic overs, while Verity, who rarely bowled a bad delivery in 446 balls (55.6 overs), finished with two for 97, with 14 maidens.

South Africa: 530 (Van der Bijl 125, Nourse 103, Melville 78, Grieveson 75, Dalton 57; Perks 5-100).

———

England replied cautiously but lost Gibb shortly before tea with the total on nine, feathering a rising delivery from Newson into the gloves of Grieveson, much to the delight of 6,000 spectators. Paynter joined Hutton at the wicket under a darkening sky, and the pair had to scrap and scrape for survival with run-scoring opportunities few and far between. Paynter took 20 minutes to get off the mark and Gordon bowled three maidens on the trot, exploiting the conditions expertly in tandem with Langton, who beat the bat on numerous occasions to draw gasps from the crowd. Hutton relieved the pressure with a couple of crisp square-cuts to the boundary before, inevitably, a combination of bad light and rain brought the third day to a close with England on 35 for one. 'It was not a good foundation for a prospective innings of over 500 runs,' Paynter remembered.

The chatter around the ground was that the momentum had started to shift in favour of the Springboks – the newspapers would certainly say as much the following morning – and batting would only get harder as the match progressed. England's first objective was to avoid the follow-on, in conditions that were expected to assist the bowlers; the weather forecast was for more humidity and cloud cover. That night the England players heard the familiar patter of rain on the streets outside their hotel, and wondered whether the pitch could repeat its powers of rejuvenation for a second day in succession.

England: 35-1, trail South Africa (530) by 495 runs.

Five

The Cut-Price Test

'By all precedents South Africa were already in a winning position' – Louis Duffus

Day four: Tuesday, 7 March

There was the usual huddle of spectators and groundstaff crowded around the middle before the start of play on the fourth day, indulging in what had already become one of the timeless Test's many rituals: diagnosing the state of the wicket. Made from a rich clay-like soil extracted from the nearby Umgeni River, the wicket had one enduring quality: it knitted together in the wet and rolled out as good as new. Despite the previous night's downpour, the strip remained unmarked after three punishing rounds. Once more, the corner men had worked their magic.

Indeed, far from hastening the conclusion of the Test, as many had predicted, the rain appeared to be protracting it. 'The pitch was soft, but the heavy roller was used twice before play started and ironed out the surface,' Duffus reported. Not that England's batsmen were expecting a comfortable ride. The breeze had died away but there was a canopy of clouds and moisture in the air to aid the bowlers, especially Gordon and Langton. 'The prediction was that, without further rain, the pitch would assist the bowlers for an hour or so and then become plumb,' Duffus added. If the Springboks were going to knock over the batsmen quickly and enforce the follow-on, they would need to make their incursions early, while the conditions remained in their favour. Instead, England handed them a wicket on a plate.

There were only a few hundred spectators in the ground when Newson bowled the first over to Paynter, though as ever those numbers would swell later in the day, or sooner if South Africa made a sensational start. Newson had trouble locating the stumps with his first six balls but the seventh thudded into Paynter's pads and the left-hander survived a concerted appeal for leg-before. Langton bowled a typically testing spell to Hutton and runs came sporadically, only nine in the first half-hour. 'Hutton and Paynter were soon patting and prodding at the pitch when back at the old address this morning,' Pollock wrote. The pair had added a further 20 runs to the total, and were still treating the wicket with a mixture of suspicion and the utmost caution, when Hutton, on 38, played a ball from Gordon to Van der Bijl at mid-on and moved purposefully out of his crease. Paynter responded immediately and was halfway down the wicket before his partner shouted, 'No,' but the little Lancastrian kept coming and Van der Bijl's return to Gordon left Hutton stranded in the middle of the track. 'It was a deplorable business,' Pollock judged. 'Paynter could have got safely back if he had done what Hutton told him to.'

Hammond's arrival at the wicket on 64 for two did little to accelerate the scoring rate, or suggest permanence. He was not at his best and spent almost 30 minutes marooned on three, tied down by the bowling of Gordon, who swung the ball dangerously late from an exacting length. Gordon had delivered a similarly awkward spell to the England captain in the fourth Test in Johannesburg, and Nourse declared that it was the first time he had seen Hammond look worried at the crease: 'To watch him in acute discomfort was a new experience for me.'

At the other end Paynter was performing his own go-slow, neglecting all but the easiest scoring opportunities, aware that his first objective was to keep his wicket intact. It was during this pivotal point in the game that Melville's undemonstrative but shrewd captaincy gained in authority. His attacking field changes and placings, made with no more than a barely discernible movement of the finger, like a secret sign, were instantly spotted by his fielders and eagerly acted on; their returns, whipped in over the top of the stumps to Grieveson, intensified the pressure on the batsmen.

Hammond grew increasingly impatient. He had failed to despatch a single boundary and, after taking the score to 125 and completing a 50-run partnership with Paynter after lunch, he skipped down the wicket to Dalton's leg-spin, drove at fresh air and was stumped by Grieveson for 24. It was a quicksilver piece of work, Duffus pointed out, 'as the ball had been deflected by the batsman's pads'. Ames's uncluttered approach to batting perfectly mirrored his wicketkeeping and he announced himself with a couple of confident straight drives to the ropes after replacing Hammond. As Duffus duly noted, 'There was no occasion during the tour when Ames did not play bold enterprising cricket.'

Paynter, though, struggled on. He was dropped in the slips by Melville off the luckless Gordon on 46 and beaten time and again outside off stump, before eventually reaching his half-century in 220 minutes – slower than it had taken Van der Bijl and Nourse to compile theirs. He had been unable to throw off the cares of timeless cricket and, for a batsman who invariably brought a blast of fresh air with him to the wicket, it was an innings played entirely against type: stale and flat. After adding 44 with Ames, however, his luck ran out and he was trapped in front by a Langton off-cutter, having struck only three boundaries in his 62. At 169 for four, with the ground slowly starting to fill up, Edrich walked out to the middle with more than just a hint of crisis in the air.

Two runs later his wretched Test form continued when he was deceived by a cleverly disguised slower ball from Langton, played too soon and prodded it straight to Rowan at silly mid-on, who devoured the catch. Edrich admitted he had been so consumed by nerves during his short stay that it was like batting under 'a black shadow'. His confidence was shot: 'I could not see the ball properly; I felt for it desperately . . .' He was replaced at the wicket by Valentine – a batsman, conversely, with enough chutzpah to supply an entire team and still have some left over. The crisis swiftly turned into an adventure, and for the first time in the match the scoring rate romped above a run a minute. The Kent pair contributed 58 in 55 minutes to the total, bringing 'a reviving breath of festival Canterbury to the solemnities', as the inimitable R. C. Robertson-Glasgow phrased it in *Wisden*[1].

They enjoyed themselves so much they did not even bother to appeal against the fading light, and Ames bustled to his half-century in 97 minutes. Duffus observed how they 'scampered up and down the wicket as though competing in a race against time . . . indulging in cheerful banter'.

It could not last, of course, and with the total on 229, Valentine's cameo came to an end at 26 when he overreached himself against Dalton, dancing down the track to become Grieveson's second stumping victim of the innings and the sixth England wicket to fall. Dalton bowled Verity for three soon after – 245 for seven – with a ball that dipped and turned but Ames continued to play a brilliant hand, taking 11 off one Dalton over, before even he conceded it was too dark to carry on. When play was again suspended early for the day, Ames was unbeaten on 82 and England were teetering at 268 for seven. 'It was significant,' Pollock concluded, 'that the only England batsman who really batted in his ordinary, normal fashion, Leslie Ames, came off best.'

England: 268-7 (Ames 82no, Paynter 62) trail South Africa (530) by 262 runs.

Day five: Wednesday, 8 March
Admission prices had been reduced by the time the game ticked over into its fifth day. The announcements,

made during the previous day's play, rang and reverberated around a ground that was often barely half-full, despite South Africa's commanding position. The crowds had declined significantly since Saturday's pinnacle of 11,000, and the public address announcements lent a somewhat farcical quality to proceedings. The absurdity of the situation was certainly not lost on Pollock. 'It has been broadcast that if the match goes beyond Tuesday, the prices of admission will be reduced,' he wrote, before adding: 'The announcer omitted to say on Tuesday of what week.' His humour remained as indestructible as the pitch itself.

Further reductions followed during Wednesday's play, prompting one South African newspaper to suggest that the timeless Test should be renamed 'the cut-price Test'. Pollock mused whether a game in which only one side had completed a full innings in four days, and the public already appeared to have given up on, was not becoming 'a sort of bargain sale'. Despite this, the receipts for the first five days of the timeless Test would realise £3,640 – a record for Kingsmead.

Ames, who had at least given the crowd their money's worth on Tuesday in an innings that radiated class, added only two more runs to his overnight score when play resumed in warm sun and a gentle sea breeze. No more than 500 spectators had taken advantage of the admission reduction when Ames, attempting to hit his eighth boundary, drove Langton fiercely on the up into the covers, where Dalton leapt and pulled off a breathtaking two-handed catch. 'It seemed that Melville just touched the ball as it flew past him at silly mid-off,' Duffus reported. It was a hammer blow for England, whose chances of beating the follow-on, slim at best, disappeared with Ames. Farnes and Wright, however, used the long handle to good effect, taking the score past 300, before Newson and Dalton – with his fourth wicket of the innings – delivered the final thrust. England were bowled out for 316, made in seven hours and 38 minutes in what had amounted to an anxious and fragmented performance.

England: 316 (Ames 84; Dalton 4-59) trail South Africa (530) by 214 runs.

———

Bob Crisp, the former South African fast bowler, adventurer and twice conqueror of Mount Kilimanjaro, turned Fleet Street journalist, judged that England were already a beaten side. 'Their fall is imminent,' he wrote, with his usual unassailable confidence in the *Daily Mail* on Wednesday morning. 'Even allowing for all the traditional uncertainties of cricket, it seems impossible that they can extricate themselves from their difficult position.' Melville, he added, was unlikely to enforce the follow-on – 'That would be foolish except on a sticky wicket' – and concluded: 'But if we cannot tell you when it will end, we can tell you how it will end, in the defeat of England.'[2]

Melville, as predicted, did not enforce the follow-on, despite a lead of 214. The South African captain, who had spent much of England's innings carrying a leg injury, dropped himself down the order instead, sending in Mitchell in his place to open with Van der Bijl. Or to put it another way, as Robertson-Glasgow did, 'Melville was dead lame. But he could still speak. So on they went.' Pollock observed that the game was already taking its toll on the players, and 'some of the South Africans had looked just about done in this fifth morning. Melville's right leg was so stiff that it took him a long time to cross over between overs, and Van der Bijl evidently found it difficult to run or bend'. According to Nourse the prospect of putting England in again had not even been up for discussion: 'This was an opportunity for piling on the agony and making perfectly certain of victory by leaving England an impossible total in the final innings when the wicket must be showing signs of wear.'

Hammond disagreed and believed that by foregoing the chance to make England bat again, Melville had made a blunder he would come to regret. 'We might have lost the match if we had done so, for we were tired and the pitch was not too good,' he commented later. 'There is always a disheartening feeling about following on in a Test.'

The wicket, in fact, was starting to display its first battle scars, where the footmarks of the bowlers had left a tracery of scratches and scuff marks, but the turf remained iron-hard, still packed with runs. Reunited as an opening pair, Mitchell and Van der Bijl gave South Africa's second innings the perfect launch, quickly removing the sting from England's opening attack and rubbing in their dominance at every opportunity. Things had not augured well for England from the moment the ball slipped from Farnes's grasp as he was about to propel the first delivery, and his return bout with Van der Bijl did not materialise. Perks even resorted to releasing the ball from some two or three yards behind the bowling crease, just for the sake of trying something different or to combat the boredom, and Ames was soon standing up to the stumps to both fast men. 'Van der Bijl, with his old enemy Farnes reduced to medium pace or resting in the sun instead of buffeting him with fast bumpers, scored more quickly than Mitchell,' Pollock reported.

At one point a voice in the crowd boomed out: 'You'll still be here at Christmas.' The bleak image seemed to stick inside the heads of the fielders and two chances went astray; Wright was the unfortunate bowler on both occasions. Verity spilled the first, reprieving Van der Bijl at short-leg though, as Pollock suggested, 'he did not appear to be fully awake . . . He wasn't the only one in that state by a long chalk'. A little later Paynter, fielding in the same position, put down a relatively simple chance from Mitchell. The half-century stand arrived in 65 minutes, and when the score reached 86 the Springboks were 300 ahead and work on another mighty foundation was well under way. 'By all precedents South Africa were already in a winning position,' Duffus insisted.

Van der Bijl was the first to his half-century after 124 minutes, and Mitchell reached his soon after, twice square-cutting loose deliveries from Wright to the boundary; the 150 came up in 187 minutes. Farnes, whose battles with both men raged long and hard during the series, was ungrudging in his praise for the opening pair. His repeated attempts to blast Van der Bijl from the crease may have strayed over the line on occasion but had been countered, he readily acknowledged, by a batsman with the heart of a prizefighter. 'He played with great determination and concentration,' he wrote in *Tours and Tests*. 'An excellent judge of the ball to leave alone, he was very hard to shift indeed, and moved across the wicket to play the ball farther than anyone I have seen. Being slow-footed he was expected to be prey for the spinners, but had generally the better of them.' His remarks typified the respect and high regard that the teams formed for each other's abilities. It was Mitchell's wicket, though, that Farnes prized above all others: 'When I consider South Africa's batting, Mitchell stands out in my mind as the dominating figure. At times he was painfully slow, and probably felt his responsibility greatly. But he was always so sound, and stands upright at the crease, gently swaying his bat with a quiet, reserved indolence.'

Like Nourse, Mitchell experienced a somewhat unconventional introduction to cricket but one that was no less inspiring. He learned to bat on a dust-covered road next to the vacant lots of a Johannesburg gold mine, surrounded by its vast mountains of excavated earth. There, he faced the bowling of his elder sister with just a tin can for a wicket, the back garden of the family cottage being too small for the purposes of cricket. At the age of six he was spotted by the former South African wicketkeeper E. A. Halliwell, who boldly predicted that he would play for his country before he reached 20. Halliwell was only five months out with his prophecy: Mitchell made his Test debut in June 1929 at Birmingham, scoring 88 and an unbeaten 61 against an England attack that boasted the likes of Harold Larwood and Maurice Tate.

That his sister was the most profound influence on his formative years, however, is not in doubt; he could not have had a more proficient teacher. Talented enough to earn a place in the women's XI at the Wanderers Club as a more than handy bat, she also impressed on her brother the qualities of sportsmanship for which he later became so admired. What he didn't learn about batting from his sister he gleaned from a book, and not just any book: it was the first he owned and was written by the batting idol of the day, Jack Hobbs. As Duffus remarked: 'If it were possible to point to one batsman after whom Mitchell modelled his style, for he has many strokes peculiarly his own, then that batsman would be Jack Hobbs. When he is not wholly on defence, Mitchell exalts the craft of batsmanship.'

If so he kept it well hidden on this occasion, and though South Africa were now in complete command, neither he nor Van der Bijl showed any inclination to force the pace or chance their arm. Instead they stuck rigidly to the script of dragging out England's pain for as long as they could, and continued to grind remorselessly on. Duffus calculated that after tea, with the lead steadily mounting towards 400 and the faster bowlers unable to raise a gallop, 'the time was ripe to thrash the tired attack'. In the final analysis it would appear that this was one of several missed opportunities by both sides to irrevocably alter the course of the game, or to send the equivalent of a thousand volts surging through it. Unfortunately, the mindset that dictates a team must score as many runs as possible to win a timeless Test, no matter how slowly, too often exerted a numbing effect on the majority of the batsmen – the venturesome Ames and Valentine apart. Certainly, the rattle of three quick wickets shortly before the close might have given Van der Bijl and Mitchell cause to regret their dilatory approach.

The pair had nudged South Africa's lead over 400, topping an aggregate of a thousand runs for the match in the process, when Mitchell trod on his stumps, executing a back-foot drive off Verity having made 89 out of an opening partnership of 191. After almost four hours without a wicket it was a rare moment of delight and relief for England; and, as so often happens after ending a long stand, they proceeded to capture two more in quick succession. Doug Wright, interviewed about the match 43 years later, referred to it as an extraordinary passage of play: 'Most people were probably dozing in the evening sun, perhaps thinking of returning home, when suddenly it all happened . . .'

The next man in, Rowan, appeared and disappeared in the space of three balls, subtly deceived by a slower delivery from Verity, before Wright himself removed Van der Bijl in the next over without addition to the score – three runs short of becoming the first South African to make two hundreds in a Test. At the start of the over Wright had served up a full toss that just begged to be clattered to the boundary. Nourse, who was batting at the other end, recalled that, 'Van der Bijl was so astonished at the sight of a full toss coming at him that he did not know what to do with it. He patted it back instead. Two balls later, he was caught at short square-leg trying to do what he should have done to the full toss.' Paynter was the fielder and threw the ball high into the air, hardly able to believe his luck. Van der Bijl had batted for 230 minutes and struck seven fours, but missed out on the one that mattered. South Africa plunged from 191-0 to 191-3 in the space of barely two overs. 'No doubt Van der Bijl will remember that unpunished full toss as long as he lives,' Duffus reflected.

England and Wright might have bagged another before the close but Hammond, fielding at mid-off, could not cling on to a drive of bludgeoning power from Nourse that streaked towards him out of the evening shadows.

South Africa: 530 & **193-3** (Van der Bijl 97, Mitchell 89) lead England (316) by 407 runs.

Day six: Thursday, 9 March

Ironically, after that late flurry of wickets, South Africa made what was their most assertive start of the game when play resumed on the sixth day. Already trailing by a monstrous 407 runs, and with the prospect of more to come, England found themselves in the desperate position of having to amass a record fourth-innings score to win the match. Although they held the record for the highest last-innings total in a Test at that time – 411 against Australia at Sydney in 1924 – it had been mustered in a losing cause. Melville could not have put it any better when he said, 'If England can win, I am ready to congratulate them on cricket's greatest feat ever.'

The overnight pair, Nourse and Viljoen, were swiftly into their stride, setting a tempo that never slackened on a 'gruelling hot day with the heavy humid atmosphere typical of a Durban summer'. There was another small crowd in, no more than between 300 or 400, Duffus estimated. The players had become used to the smattering of spectators who attended those often eerily quiet pre-lunch sessions. 'Despite the fact that the match was considered to have become dreadfully dull, there were always five or six thousand present by the afternoon,' the journalist reiterated. Happily, he continued, the verdict of most Durbanites was not reflected in the rest of the country; the distance seemed to lend the timeless Test an appeal all of its own:

> For those who watched the game day after day, it was at times a wearisome affair, but to the thousands of people all over Southern Africa who heard or read the scores in intervals, through broadcasts, newspapers or word passed hourly through countless city offices, it was the most absorbing match of all. In Johannesburg, or in Cape Town a thousand miles away, there was much more enthusiasm than round the field at Durban.

Viljoen tucked away the first ball of the morning, bowled by Wright, for a comfortable single, and Nourse drilled the second to the boundary with a rasping square-cut; he then pulled the eighth so ferociously to the fence that it caused Edrich to duck hurriedly to the ground at short-leg, the Kent leg-spinner opening with his familiar medley of long-hops and unplayable deliveries. When Farnes, back at full bore after his brief guise as a medium-paced trundler the previous day, dug one in short at Nourse, it received the same treatment: a thunderous hook struck the fence with such explosive force that Pollock reported he half-expected to see it disintegrate in a shower of sparks. Jackie McGlew wrote of Nourse that, because his follow-through was negligible and his backswing so short, 'spectators were often amazed at the speed with which the ball would rocket to the boundary'. With 34 added in the first half-hour, South Africa had regained the initiative and England's predicament appeared more forlorn with every run.

Nourse was in his element but, having put on a rapid 51 with Viljoen, he allowed exuberance to get the better of him. In attempting to repeat the hook off Farnes, he mistimed the shot, sending the ball high into the air but at no great distance, and Hutton completed the catch close to the wicket. Nourse's departure for 25 did nothing to stem the flow of runs, however. Melville looked in some discomfort with his injured leg but did not consider himself inconvenienced enough to use a runner, and was soon threading the ball through the gaps and leaning into some silky cover-drives.

After lunch, with the Springboks having increased their lead to 506, Perks pretended to crawl back to the field on his hands and knees, much to the amusement of the few hundred spectators. England finally separated Melville and Viljoen – who rivalled each other for timing and elegance during a stand of 104 – when the latter, having made 74, played on to a ball from Perks, whose ability to hurry the batsman even on this wicket was no mean achievement. Despite the immensity of the task confronting the tourists, they never veered from the high standard they set for themselves in the field, a couple of fumbled catches aside. Ames was as polished as ever behind the stumps and the pace and determination at which Paynter chased the ball in the deep, the accuracy and length of his throwing, astonished the spectators. 'Their morale was amazing,' Duffus acknowledged.

They had also been in the field since before lunch on the previous day and, when Dalton walked out to replace Viljoen at 346 for five, it was to be greeted by the sight of all 11 fielders, and one of the umpires, sitting or sprawled full-length on the grass. Dalton contributed a breezy 21 that included a six onto the grandstand roof off Wright, giving the players another welcome excuse to flop down on the turf. 'The field had a nice sit-down,' Pollock reported, 'until some busybody retrieved the ball and made them all get up again.'

Hammond made his 25th bowling change of the game when he whistled up Hutton for an over of leg-spin, before Wright disposed of Dalton soon after with an agile catch off his own bowling, plucking a crunching straight drive off his bootlaces. Moments later Verity was convinced he had snaffled another when he bowled a ball that appeared to graze Grieveson's bat before lodging in Ames's pads. So convinced that he had got his man, in fact, he appealed not once but three times. At the third time of asking, Verity turned to the umpire and said, 'I'm appealing for a catch at the wicket,' and for the third time the umpire informed the bowler, 'Not out.' The rules state: 'The striker is out if the ball is "hugged to the body of the catcher", even though he has not touched it with his hands. Should the ball lodge in the fieldsman's clothing, or in the top of the wicketkeeper's pads, this will amount to its being "hugged to the body of the catcher".'

Verity's quiet manner of appealing was as much a feature of his cricket as his high classical action, variety of pace, unwavering line and length and easy seven-pace run-up. It was said that his appeals were so quiet that 'only the umpire and batsman at his end could hear him'. His fellow Yorkshireman, the fast-medium Bill Bowes, remembered his 'nice enquiry', adding, 'He didn't scream his head off or throw his arms up, like some of us did.' Hutton wrote of him, 'there was no sharp practice', while Jack Fingleton recalled that his appeals made 'with fingers cupped to mouth' were invariably followed by a wry smile and a wink to the batsman. It was rare for Verity – the most phlegmatic and fair-minded of men – to display even the slightest emotion on the field, let alone to appeal three times in the same breath. Equally, he would not let the incident rankle; he returned briskly to his mark, eager to complete the job in hand, there were four more wickets still to take.

Hammond, just as the England captains Douglas Jardine, Bob Wyatt and 'Gubby' Allen had done before him, knew exactly what to expect every time he threw Verity the ball: artistry, accuracy, reliability and imperturbability. But he was more than just the patient pivot of England's attack. He was, as his Australian spin rival 'Tiger' O'Reilly described him, 'the essence of a team man'. There was not a young player, either on tour with England or at Yorkshire, who did not benefit from his encouragement and generosity of spirit. Hutton, whose admiration for Verity knew no bounds, said, 'Hedley was always willing to come out and bowl at me in the nets for ten minutes . . . Nothing seemed too much trouble for him.' Hugh Bartlett told the author Alan Hill how he 'took him under his wing' during those early days on tour in South Africa, and was always passing on tips to help him improve his batting: 'Hedley was a marvellous, steadying influence on people.' There was about him a calming presence and quiet wisdom – 'his natural dignity', Hutton called it – all the qualities that would make him such an outstanding officer when the time came, as Verity knew it would.

In fact, the threat of war and the quickening beat of martial drums were as much a part of the timeless Test as every run scored and every wicket taken. The inevitable chatter about war among spectators, interspersed with the shrill cries of the newspaper boys, did not go unnoticed out in the middle and provided a constant accompaniment to the sounds of the cricket. The England players listened to the latest news bulletins and voraciously consumed every newspaper they could lay their hands on, though they did not make for comfortable reading. Thousands of air-raid shelters had already been delivered to homes throughout Britain, solidifying the players' view that war was inevitable. The civic defence of London and the recruitment and training of ARP wardens had been under way for months; the expression 'war effort' was much in use; the plans for the evacuation of a million or more children from the capital were in readiness.

The snail's pace of the cricket contrasted graphically with the terrifying speed in which events were unfolding some 5,000 miles away, highlighting the absurdity and the futility of the timeless Test. The words 'unreal' and 'dreamlike' were often used by the players in the coming days and weeks, and it wasn't difficult to see why. At times it felt as if they were operating in a vacuum or, at worst, as if they were perpetuating a charade – one that was no nearer reaching a conclusion, despite having entered its sixth day.

After his early scare against Verity, Grieveson spent a tiresome 40 minutes attempting to get off the mark but stuck with his captain while he kept the scoreboard ticking over at the other end. When South Africa reached tea on 387 for six they had accumulated a lead of 601, and were for all intents and purposes out of sight. England re-emerged for the final session with Gibb wearing the gloves. Ames, whose work behind the stumps was a triumph of sustained focus and skill, conceding only six byes while South Africa hoarded 917 runs, took a well-deserved rest in the outfield.

During this time Melville advanced swiftly through the nineties, striking three effortless boundaries in an over off Wright, and reached a maiden Test century in 199 minutes with what was described as 'a storm of cheering' from some 3,000 spectators. It took an exceptional ball to dismiss him, and Farnes produced it, trimming his off stump with a fast outswinger to end a graceful and commanding innings of 103. Bowling flat out Farnes then rounded up the tail, having Langton magnificently caught at slip by Hammond – who proved that almost two days of unremitting concentration in the field had not dulled his reflexes – and flattened the leg stump of the obdurate Grieveson for 39.

The Springboks were all out for 481, leaving England with 'a mere 696 to win the match', as Paynter put it, though it is possible he phrased it somewhat more colourfully than that. Verity bowled 766 balls in all – 17 more than Somerset's Jack White, another left-arm spinner, managed against Australia at Adelaide in 1929 – to return the remarkable match figures of 95.6-23-184-4. Farnes's second-inning's efforts were rewarded with a highly respectable four for 74 from 22.1 overs.

South Africa: 481 (Melville 103, Van der Bijl 97, Mitchell 89, Viljoen 74; Farnes 4-74).

———

England still had a potentially nerve-jangling five minutes to negotiate before the close, but faced only one ball, from Newson, after Hutton's appeal against the fading light was upheld. For the sixth evening in succession the stumps were pulled early and England's opening pair could not get off the field fast enough, almost as if they feared that the umpires might suddenly change their minds.

England: 316 & **0-0** need 696 runs to beat **South Africa: 530** & **481**.

Six

The Long Reply

'If it was batting they wanted, we were a batting side' – Walter Hammond

Day seven: Friday, 10 March

It was a week since Hammond led England on to the Kingsmead pitch for the start of the timeless Test, with what Duffus remembered as 'a fresh ambitious spirit'; a week, 1,327 runs and 30 wickets, since Farnes bowled the first ball to Van der Bijl on a sunlit morning, before a noisy and expectant crowd of several thousand. Now, on the second Friday of the match, it was muggy and overcast with the threat of thunder and, though admission fees had been waived for the rest of the game (it appeared that even the officials had all but washed their hands of it), there were still precious few spectators.

A Test that was supposed to have lasted only five days had spectacularly surpassed all expectations in terms of its longevity, aided and abetted by a pitch that, in the words of Pollock, refused 'to grow old gracefully'. The *Natal Mercury*, attempting to drum up any last vestiges of interest, offered a cash prize of five guineas to the reader who could correctly predict its date of completion. When Hutton and Gibb returned to the middle to embark on 'England's hopeless task', as one South African newspaper triumphantly headlined it, there were no more than a hundred or so regulars occupying their favourite seats – all of whom were content only for the match to run and run.

That morning before the start of play the England side had taken their usual stroll from their hotel to the ground. 'By now we not only knew the way but many of the shop-keepers and people living on the route. After all, it was the seventh day,' Wright recalled. 'A fair amount of good-humoured banter passed between us regarding the 696 runs we needed. No one gave us the slightest chance.' Yet England remained undaunted; they were not a side easily demoralised or deflated. How could they be anything other when they possessed strokemakers of such dazzling fluency and attacking disposition as Hammond, Ames, Hutton, Paynter and Valentine? Tired as they were, they were determined to back themselves in the face of such seemingly insuperable odds. As *Wisden* remarked: 'Few people imagined they had a ghost of a chance of averting defeat, much less of scoring such a colossal total.'

Hammond was only too aware that to play anxiously would be to play into South Africa's hands and, as long as the pitch continued to sap the bowlers' strength and didn't suddenly turn into a raging powder-keg, he believed England had nothing to fear. To this end he openly encouraged the batsmen to be positive and to play their natural game. Later that morning he would shuffle the England batting order – another courageous call that was to have considerable impact on the bearing of the game. 'No side has ever won a match with a total like that against them in the final innings, but we intended to give it a try. If it was batting they wanted, we were a batting side,' he insisted. It was paramount that Hutton and Gibb gave England a solid start, and the Yorkshire pair carried out Hammond's instructions to the letter.

Hutton gave an indication of what was to come in the first over, twice driving Langton through the covers to get the scoreboard moving and immediately looked in supreme touch. Langton, handicapped by a strapped back, was one of several players already feeling the diminishing toll of the past six days, and for the first time in the series he struggled to control his line. The bowler whom Melville invariably turned to in a crisis would finish the match 'lame and at half-pace' after ploughing his way through 56 second-innings overs for a solitary wicket. Dalton, the partnership-breaker *par excellence*, was swiftly introduced but could make little impression on Hutton, who continued to score at every opportunity, quite impervious to the dangers of the situation.

Gibb, scampering quick singles and nudging the ball cleverly into the gaps, proved the perfect foil for his more adventurous partner and England's 50 was posted in 70 minutes. Hutton's half-century followed 12 minutes later, with his fifth boundary. He appeared set fair for his first hundred of the series when, ten minutes before lunch, he aimed a cut at an innocuous leg-break from Mitchell and smeared the ball into his stumps for 55 – one of half a dozen batsmen to lose his wicket in that manner during the game. It was a sorry end to an innings that promised so much, and he banged his bat angrily into the ground before departing. At 78 for one Hammond sprung a surprise, and it was not the jaunty figure of Paynter who emerged down the pavilion steps and out into the middle, but Edrich.

Hammond argued that Edrich's lack of Test runs was more to do with ill-luck than poor form, and his advice to the all-rounder before pushing him up the order had been simple: 'Don't be afraid to go for the ball, Bill.' Despite an average of only 4.02 for the series and a reputation among the South Africans as a walking wicket, Hammond was convinced that he could make good. Only the day before he had received a cable from his fellow Middlesex reveller and swashbuckler Denis Compton, offering him similar encouragement, and he slipped it in his pocket before going out to bat. On the players' balcony it was noticeable that the Springboks exchanged glances – one or two expressed wry amusement, some of the crowd even sniggered – as Edrich made his way to the wicket. 'It was quite evident that they felt Hammond's gamble, at this crucial stage of the match, had provided them with a proverbial "lamb to the slaughter",' Paynter recounted.

Mitchell was waiting for Edrich at the bowler's end with a wide grin, tossing the ball impatiently from hand to hand in his eagerness to get at him. 'The grin finished me,' Edrich wrote, but he kept repeating Hammond's words in his head. Mitchell's first ball pitched on leg stump and Edrich drove it confidently, straight out of the middle of the bat, past mid-on to the boundary. He played the same stroke an over later, watching the ball ripple across the turf to the fence, and remembered that it felt 'as if I had taken a large dose of strong tonic'.

In fact, there was more than just a dose of tonic coursing through Edrich's veins. The previous night he had attended a party thrown by another Middlesex adventurer, the former South African batsman 'Tuppy' Owen-Smith, at the Athlone Gardens nightclub, just a rickshaw ride away from the team hotel[1]. It was no secret that the outgoing Edrich enjoyed a party and a drink or two, and his decision to subject himself to 'a regime of early nights and strictly rationed drinking and smoking' in an effort to heighten his game and eradicate the mistakes would have required a serious amount of willpower on his part. On tour in India with Lionel Tennyson's X1 a year earlier, his 'bohemian jollities' had not gone down well at Lord's and prompted a written reprimand. By adopting a more sedate routine, Edrich had commuted the element of danger and risk on which he thrived.

On the night of Owen-Smith's party he no doubt reasoned he had nothing left to lose – after all, his form couldn't get any worse – and he proceeded to tear up the rule book in style. As his biographer Alan Hill explained: 'He drank freely. It lasted until the early hours of the morning, and it was a champagne tonic for Edrich's flagging spirits. He forgot all his worries amid the camaraderie of the party.' He was so worse for wear that his team-mates had to put him to bed that morning, but 'he was smiling when they shook him awake . . .'

He was still smiling when he passed his previous highest Test score of 28, with a fortunate snick to the boundary off Gordon, and soon overhauled Gibb. 'The South Africans began to trek out into the great open spaces away from the wicket,' Hammond noted with a glow of pride. His powers restored, Edrich farmed the strike and celebrated a maiden Test half-century with his eighth boundary in 99 minutes, the fourth quickest of the game after Hutton (82 minutes), Dalton (95) and Ames (97). Like Gibb, he would not perhaps win any prizes for elegance but his uncomplicated methods proved hugely effective and he was always in his element in a battle. Predominantly an on-side player the keynotes to his batting were his unflinching courage – one writer called it a 'nonchalant contempt for danger' – his wonderful eye and pugnacity, fortified by the sturdiest of defences. He was also a ferocious and fearless hooker of fast bowling, who would rather take a blow than a backward step, drove heartily and played the late cut as well as anyone. The eminent sports columnist Ian Wooldridge perfectly captured the essence of the man when he wrote:

> Bill Edrich epitomised the particularly British breed of incurable scallywag. He loved life too much to harbour grudges, sustain feuds, or niggle

opponents with whom, like as not, he'd be out on the tiles at the close of play. But there was a bottom line to all this roistering. You had to be there before the start of play, next day. Then, hungover or otherwise, you had to fight . . .

As ever, Gibb continued to sell his wicket dearly and was the bulwark at the other end while the partnership burgeoned. Nicknamed 'Gibbralter' by the South African crowds for his rock-like presence at the crease, he also provided spectators with a constant source of amusement. 'His very zeal made him an addict of idiosyncrasies,' Duffus wrote, whether it was repeatedly adjusting his sleeves or glasses while he waited for the bowler to run in, batting in a white tennis eyeshade to the amusement of the crowd, or swishing imaginary drives at the non-striker's end to 'refresh his memory of a stroke that might be otherwise forgotten'. A steady drizzle during the afternoon caused his glasses to steam up, and at one point after stopping the game to appeal to Melville and the umpires about the conditions, he made off towards the pavilion only to double back when he realised that the rest of the players – including Edrich – had decided to stay on the field. By this stage Gibb's eccentricities had become almost second nature to his team-mates, and even it seemed the Springboks.

Edrich continued to dominate the strike after tea, moving ever closer to a century despite Melville taking the tenth new ball of the game. The crowd had swollen to at least 4,000 by this time and was cheering, whistling and clapping his every run. He reached 99 with a drive for two off Langton and completed his milestone with a comfortable single in the same over – courtesy of a misfield by the bowler – and was soaking up the applause before he reached the other end. He had struck 12 boundaries and batted for three hours and 13 minutes to end one of the most fraught baptisms in Test history. 'There was an enormous reception,' Norman Preston recorded in *Wisden*. 'The crowd gave him an ovation, the South Africans congratulated him and high up on the balcony shouts of triumph came from his comrades.'

There was acclaim, too, for Hammond's 'masterly stroke of leadership' in elevating Edrich. The England captain rarely allowed himself to act on a hunch, but on this occasion it had paid off handsomely. 'Probably it is not an exaggeration to say Edrich's whole cricket future hung on success or failure today,' Pollock reported. 'But he rewarded his captain, and did himself an incalculable turn by coming to light with a real cricketer's innings.' No wonder, either, that Edrich wrote later of Hammond's call, 'It was the stuff of which great captains are made.'

When bad light ended play at 5.40 p.m. England were 253 for one, with Edrich on 107 and Gibb 78; in putting on 175 the pair had whittled away South Africa's lead to 443. 'The odds are still very much on the Springboks winning the game,' Jack Gage, the cricket correspondent of the *Daily Tribune*, filed that evening. However, he acknowledged that by their refusal to yield so much as an inch, England had not just created doubt in the minds of the South Africans for the first time in the match, but awarded themselves 'an outside chance of pulling off what would be the most sensational Test win in cricket history'. Then came the rain.

England: 316 & **253-1** (Edrich 107no, Gibb 78no, Hutton 55) require 443 runs to beat **South Africa: 530** & **481**.

Day eight: Saturday, 11 March

As much as half an inch of rain fell overnight, but it had eased off to a drizzle again by Saturday morning when the teams arrived at the ground. At first the Springboks believed it to be the answer to their prayers. 'When we woke up to see the rain drizzling down, we thought we had the match in the bag,' Grieveson confessed. Although the heavy roller had been used to dry the surface, the contention was that the uncovered wicket would retain enough moisture to assist the bowlers and enable them to work their mischief. Nourse was convinced that 'there would be some fun and games at last'. However, after much urgent pacing of the dressing-room while they waited for the drizzle to subside and the sun to come out, the South Africans had their hopes dashed by another torrential downpour. Once more the wicket was swamped and at 2.40 p.m. on the eighth scheduled day of the match, following an inspection by both captains, play had to be abandoned without a ball being bowled.

By now the tourists' valedictory fixture against Western Province at Newlands was supposed to have been under way but, as with so much to do with the timeless Test, it had long since gone by the board. The *Athlone Castle* had already steamed out of Durban without the players, bound for Cape Town on the first leg of her return journey to England, while they were still in the field. 'The captain, just to let us know he was sailing, sounded three farewell blasts on the ship's siren as if to say, "I'll see you in Cape Town,"' Wright recalled. That had been on the Thursday, during the sixth playing day of the match. The mail boat was booked to depart Cape Town for Southampton on Friday, 17 March, and no one in their right mind wanted to still be playing then. 'Suggestions that had been made facetiously earlier in the week that England might have difficulty in catching the boat home – Cape Town was two days' journey away by rail – were now a reality,' Duffus remarked. 'The timeless Test was running out of time.'

Day nine: Monday, 13 March

The fickle weather continued to impose its own test on the players and Kingsmead was bathed in scorching sunshine, fanned by a cooling sea breeze, when they clocked in again for the second Monday of the match. Saturday's washout and Sunday's rest day had, in effect, provided them with an additional day off and there were rumours of 'more parties – and more champagne²'. There also appeared to be a renewed public interest in the contest and almost 1,000 spectators filed into the ground for the start of play. 'The astonishing pitch came up smiling again for the eighth playing day,' Pollock reported, though he added that there were some cracks at which Edrich gazed intently during the early overs. In fact, the pitch had now entered its third incarnation of the game. It had been cut and rolled on the Sunday and, according to Grieveson, 'looked as good as it had on the first day'.

The second-wicket pair quietly played themselves in and, after establishing that there were no hidden demons in the surface, simply carried on where they had left off on Friday. A light breeze was blowing diagonally across the wicket when Newson bowled the first over to Edrich, who clipped two runs off the fifth ball and survived a confident shout for lbw off the eighth, attempting to repeat the stroke. The breeze appeared to be assisting Langton more than Newson and he bowled to Gibb with three fielders close in on the leg side. Newson was soon replaced by Gordon, who bowled to four slips in the hope that it would encourage his swing, but Gibb cut him neatly for consecutive twos. Edrich was also batting with increasing comfort and, when Melville introduced Mitchell's leg-spin, he lofted him over square-leg to the boundary, bringing up the 200-partnership in the process.

At 12.30, after batting for two minutes over six hours (he had started his innings in the gloaming on Thursday evening), Gibb flicked Gordon off his pads for a couple of runs to long-on and collected his second century of the series. Slowly but inexorably the tide was turning. Edrich passed 150 with his 18th boundary not long after and continued to lead the cavalry charge, ploughing away through the on side and testing the equanimity of the South Africans with every run. At 333 for one at lunch, having added a further 80, England were 363 away from their objective, the second-wicket partnership already worth 255 runs.

At this point Bill Ferguson, the meticulous Australian scorer, had been reduced to the last five pages of his scorebook and feared he would be unable to record the closing stages of the match. Pollock thought Ferguson's dilemma worthy of a mention in his report of the day's play, explaining that, 'the MCC scorer didn't know where to get another book.' Hammond recalled that, on all their travels together, it was the only time he had ever seen 'Fergie' agitated. 'He is an MCC institution, and has watched more big cricket, I suppose, than any other man living.' Although his official title was scorer-baggage master, it failed to do justice to the multifarious duties he performed on tour: to use the words of Duffus, he regularly doubled up as 'manager, artist, organiser, soul of efficiency and guardian genius'. He even found the time to invent cricket's wagon-wheel, the chart that illustrates in minute detail where a batsman has scored the bulk of his runs. On one occasion on tour in England, he was memorably asked by King George VI if he used an adding machine whenever Bradman went to the wicket.

He made his first tour in 1905 when he travelled to England with Joe Darling's Australians and had been following the sun without fail ever since. An indispensable presence, he was the lifeline to many a hapless cricketer on his first tour, and a source of infallible knowledge to countless journalists on deadline. 'How many maidens has Gordon bowled now, Fergie?' 'Bill, when did Gibb last score a run?' He is there in the back row of England's official team photograph in South Africa 1938–39, a suited, diminutive, silver-haired figure with stooped shoulders, the legacy of all those years bent over his scorebook in press boxes across the world. No series would have been complete without him, whether it was England, Australia, South Africa, West Indies, New Zealand or India who were doing the touring – he had accompanied them all. The fabled 'Fergie' was on his 34th tour by 1938–39, and his eighth with England: in all that time he had never lost so much as a single item of luggage … or run out of pages in his sacred scorebook[3].

Edrich and Gibb extended their partnership by a further 25 runs after lunch to set a record for any wicket in Tests between England and South Africa, eclipsing the 268 scored by Hobbs and Sutcliffe at Lord's in 1924. By now the crowd's appeals for a wicket were growing ever more insistent. Melville appeared to have missed a trick by not bowling Dalton earlier, and some of the spectators let him know. Belatedly he summoned Dalton into the attack for his first over of the day, and the all-rounder with the icy nerve responded immediately, conjuring a top-spinner out of nowhere that hurried off the surface to knock back Gibb's middle stump for 120 with the score on 358. The Kingsmead regulars had not cheered a wicket since before lunch on Friday, and the roar that greeted Gibb's dismissal was tinged with relief. The pair had added 280 and Gibb's century, occupying seven and a half hours and including just two boundaries, was the slowest recorded by an England batsman at that time. Nonetheless, Duffus hailed it as a 'masterpiece of patience and concentration'.

Hammond joined Edrich and watched approvingly while the 22-year-old continued to gorge himself; he mixed the orthodox with the improvised, repeatedly going down on one knee to sweep the waning Langton to the boundary. Hammond had started tentatively, particularly against Gordon, and survived a huge appeal for leg-before early in his innings. Gordon remained a tireless presence for South Africa, bowling unchanged for an hour at Edrich and Hammond in the broiling heat, and was the most difficult of the bowlers to put away. Farnes was an avid admirer and noted how his 'neat, well-proportioned build and easy run-up, together with his keenness and consistently good length, enabled him to bowl for long spells at just above medium pace', concluding that he was 'one of the best bowlers on either side'.

Slowly Hammond reclaimed his touch and, when Edrich swung a full toss from Dalton to the leg-side boundary, the England score passed 400. Edrich moved to 199 with further boundaries off Mitchell, before sprinting through for a quick single to reach a chanceless and nerveless double-century in six and a half hours. Three runs later, England exceeded the previous highest score in the fourth innings of a Test – their own 411 against Australia in 1924. Melville took the eleventh new ball shortly after, and at tea the scoreboard stood at 442 for two with Edrich on 215 and Hammond 34.

The England manager Jack Holmes was waiting for Edrich with a glass of champagne when he returned to the dressing-room. 'I hear you train on the stuff,' he said, unable to suppress a broad smile. Edrich removed his sodden boots and swiftly downed two glasses during the interval, admitting he was 'thoroughly fagged'. The crowd had grown substantially by this time. 'The news of England's amazing resistance had spread through the town like wildfire and office workers donned their coats and hurried out to the ground,' the *Daily Tribune* reported. Many were still arriving when Edrich, having added a further four runs since tea and offered a sharp chance to gulley, played a weary-looking shot at Langton and was caught by a diving Gordon at short-leg, who gleefully snatched the ball inches from the turf.

'The fourth flying boat to bring mail from England since the match started flew round the ground just too late to look down on Edrich's exit,' Pollock observed. He had taken his country to the brink of an astonishing victory, become the first Englishman to hit a double-hundred in the fourth innings of a Test, batted for seven hours and 20 minutes and scored exactly 100 runs in boundaries. 'He had won himself striking rehabilitation,' Duffus wrote. 'In years to come men who were boys in 1939 will pause before the trees planted by Edrich and Gibb among the honours grove and recall with wonder how they batted for nearly two days with an insatiable appetite for runs – gluttons at this unparalleled feast.'

When bad light ended play at 5.30 – an hour after Edrich's dismissal – Hammond had passed his fifth half-century of the series, chipping another 49 runs off South Africa's great edifice, in the company of Paynter. England were 496 for three at stumps, with Hammond 58 and Paynter 24, only 200 runs away from victory. At the start of the day, requiring 443 to beat South Africa, their chances had moved, in Duffus's view, from the 'impossible to the improbable'; now they were 'odds-on favourites'. 'They had scored a great psychological as well as physical triumph,' he added. The prevailing view was that England would have to suffer a collapse of fatal proportions if they were to lose it from this position.

The end was finally in sight: a fact confirmed by the South African Cricket Board, who announced that the England players would be released from the game on Tuesday evening to enable them to catch the boat train from Durban. This would allow them not only enough time to arrive in Cape Town on Friday morning and board the *Athlone Castle* before it sailed, but to complete the match. If, by some quirk of fate, it remained still unfinished by the close of play on Tuesday it would not be extended into an eleventh day, as had earlier been proposed. 'The England players' contracts expire on Friday, when they go aboard for England at Cape Town,' Pollock reported. 'Should the players be prevented from sailing, the South African Cricket Board would have to be responsible for some form of new contract.'

Jack Holmes explained later that, with the situation in Europe growing more grave by the day, it had become impossible to obtain a berth on a ship returning to England. They were all full. Had they cancelled their booking on the *Athlone Castle* and stayed to conclude the Test, they ran the risk, he pointed out, of being stranded in South Africa for several weeks at the least. Their departure could not be delayed a moment longer.

England: 316 & **496-3** (Edrich 219, Gibb 120, Hammond 58no, Hutton 55) require 200 runs to beat **South Africa: 530** & **481**.

Day ten: Tuesday, 14 March

The weather had reverted to heavy cloud and humidity for the last day of the match; there was a blustering wind, too – a sure sign, according to local weather experts, that rain was coming. One even predicted 'a race for a finish'. It would turn out to be one of the few prophesies about the timeless Test that anyone got right. However, the turnstiles clicked merrily all morning and a crowd in excess of 2,000 watched Hammond and Paynter add 82 more runs before lunch, trimming England's target to 118. Melville's defensive fields had permitted the batsmen to push the ball into the gaps and sprint their singles almost at will – a tactic at which Hammond, 'playing strokes in croquet fashion and tapping it insolently on either side of the wicket', was particularly adept. South Africa's efforts to stem the flow of runs, the *Daily Tribune* wrote, were 'like a small boy trying frantically to stop water gushing out of a tap after mischievously unscrewing the washer'.

For one brief dazzling moment during the morning the sun appeared, illuminating the ground with the sudden glare of a spotlight, before the dark clouds bustled in again. Hammond was batting responsibly and coolly, and 15 minutes after lunch he completed the sixth century of the match, his third of the series, and his 21st in Test cricket to equal Bradman's record. He did not as a rule pay great attention to statistics, but this was one that he would have been acutely aware of. He had struck only three boundaries, but his harvesting of singles and clever placement gave the impression that his innings was in perpetual motion. Paynter, though not at his impish best, had already reached his half-century – the 16th of the game – and the England score swept on towards 600. Only the rain it seemed could save South Africa from certain defeat.

It was about this time that Swanton, having just finished a stint on air, was rung up by an enthusiastic England supporter who lived at Isipingo, a beach resort some 12 miles south of Durban. The message was short and to the point: 'It's raining hard here. Please tell Mr Hammond to hurry up.' Swanton relayed the message to the England dressing-room and, using the pretext of a spare batting glove, the twelfth man, Yardley, was sent to the middle to inform the captain.

'When Hammond examined the sky and strolled over to Paynter, we knew there was going to be an attack launched,' Nourse recalled. 'Ferociously he set about the bowling.' England were now engaged in a desperate race against time. Casting thunderous glances at the sky, Hammond batted with fierce precision, as if accelerating through the gears of his favourite Jaguar. The ball purred across the turf to the boundary, one cover-drive travelled with such rapid power that no fielder moved before it struck the fence. Paynter worked the ball efficiently off his pads, pulled and cut anything short and scampered his singles. However, another factor had entered the equation: the wicket was starting to break up. For the first time in the game puffs of dust rose from a couple of powdery patches, and the occasional ball reared disconcertingly. 'The pitch was finally relinquishing its stubborn hold on life,' Duffus concluded.

Hammond and Paynter had moved the score to 611 in an atmosphere of mounting tension and excitement when Gordon, his flannels daubed in red, his shirt clinging to his back in the steamy heat after 50 second-innings overs without a wicket, belatedly reaped his reward. He bowled a ball that appeared to kick off the surface, clip the shoulder of Paynter's bat as he swung at it and fly through to Grieveson, who completed the catch at head height. Paynter, having batted 213 minutes for his 75, looked surprised to be given out.

Black clouds were massing and the light was deteriorating rapidly as Ames walked out to replace

Paynter. Considered by many to be the most technically accomplished strokemaker in the side after Hammond – in the opinion of C. B. Fry he was a 'delightfully effective player, a sort of troubadour of a batsman' – the wicketkeeper was the ideal man for such a situation. It would have held no fears for him and he was briskly off the mark with a square-cut for two. At 619 for four Gordon, armed with the twelfth new ball of the game, drew a rare false stroke from Hammond, who edged uppishly between wicketkeeper and slip to the boundary to gasps from the spectators. Gordon, concentrating his attack primarily on leg stump where the wicket was showing marked signs of wear, maintained an admirable control, and his duel with Hammond, in particular, enthralled the crowd. 'Hammond gave the impression that as long as he was at the wickets he was quite capable of scoring any runs that England might require,' Jack Gage reported in the *Daily Tribune*. When the waiters emerged at 3.15 with trays of cold drinks, the England captain impatiently waved them away.

The first spots of rain arrived soon after, and the sound of rustling raincoats and unfurling umbrellas from the spectators in the open seats was transmitted to the middle; within seconds the players were dashing from the field. The short shower caused a stoppage of six minutes and England resumed on 631 for four;

but only three more runs were added before the rain blew in again, harder this time, delaying play for a further 15 minutes. The fifth-wicket pair advanced the score to 650 after the players re-emerged for the third time, matching each other with the resonance of their strokeplay until Hammond, in his hurry to beat the rain, took one risk too many. Unable to resist a dart down the wicket at Dalton he missed a big leg-break and was exuberantly stumped by Grieveson, succumbing to the same combination for the second time in the match. He batted for five hours and 49 minutes for his 140, hitting seven boundaries to leave England just 46 runs from victory. It was an innings of 'power and majesty', Paynter declared, and only the magnificence of the South African fielding curbed the number of boundaries he struck.

The baton passed to the carefree Valentine, who nearly suffered the same fate as Hammond to his first ball. Grieveson's work with the gloves had been nothing short of a revelation, but this time he fumbled the stumping chance and Valentine breathed again. Undeterred, he jumped out to the next ball and drove it fearlessly down the ground for four. 'We'll get them before close of play tonight,' he assured Ames at the end of the over. Just two balls into the next – Gordon's 56th of the innings – the rain came back to send the players scurrying to the pavilion. This time they would not return. The intensity of the downpour engulfed the ground in semi-darkness. Within minutes the square was awash and the pavilion lights glowed fiercely through a curtain of gloom. There was no hope for it. The rain, having rejuvenated the wicket on three separate occasions to keep the game alive well beyond its natural lifespan, had saved its cruellest trick for last.

A meeting between the two captains and the South African Board of Control was hastily convened during the tea interval to discuss the next course of action, while the exhausted teams sat in the pavilion, where 36 bottles of champagne waited to be uncorked by the winners of the rubber. The board, in fact, did not arrive at a decision for almost an hour, and some of the 5,000 or so spectators drifted out of the ground without staying to hear the verdict. During that time, Duffus reported, 'a few farsighted players, sensing the end, surreptitiously looted the stumps'. One of them was Hutton, who admitted later that a stump from the timeless Test and another from the victorious third Test, also at Kingsmead, were among the keepsakes he brought back to England.

Eventually the board came to a decision and delivered it, appropriately enough with maximum dramatic effect, to lightning pyrotechnics and a drum roll of thunder: the timeless Test was abandoned as a draw. England's attempted heist of the spoils – they were 42 runs short of an earth-shaking victory when rain chased the players off the field for the last time at 3.55 – had come to nothing. The official announcement stated:

> It has been agreed by the South African Board of Control, after consultation with the two captains, that the match be abandoned. In coming to this decision, we took into consideration the fact that the England cricketers had to be in Cape Town for a reasonable number of hours to make necessary arrangements before their departure on the *Athlone Castle* on Friday, which is essential. The requisite number of hours in Cape Town would only be possible if they leave Durban at 8.05 tonight.

Melville had argued at the meeting that England should lose by default if the game was not played out the following day. His protest was laughed off by the England players. 'South Africa wanted to claim a win by default because we could not stay another month and finish the match,' Yardley quipped. According to Pollock many of the bookmakers at the ground, and those who had wagered heavily on a positive result, voiced the same objection: 'I heard bookmakers contending that England were technical losers because they did not stay to finish the match. The argument is that England "gave up". But Hammond did not abandon the match. The South African Board of Control decided on the abandonment, and took full responsibility for it.' Having already agreed that England's players would be released from the game on Tuesday evening, the board had been left with no other choice but to honour its commitment.

Perhaps the biggest losers amidst all the disputes and confusion were the Kingsmead regulars. For those who sat through all nine playing days, even braving the thunder and rain at the bitter end to hear the final verdict, it was a dismal anti-climax and many felt cheated. The journalist Jack Gage encapsulated their frustration: 'It seemed such a pity that this remarkable game should have been brought to an unsatisfactory and unnecessary conclusion when an hour, at the most an hour and a half's play, would have sufficed to bring about a definite result.'

There was a proposal that the six remaining batsmen – Ames, Valentine, Verity, Wright, Farnes and Perks – should stay behind and fly to Cape Town instead, therefore enabling the match to be completed the following day. But even that was stymied. A clause had been inserted in the England players' contracts that prohibited them from flying during the tour. 'They were far too precious to be allowed in the air,'

Swanton divulged. Nonetheless the ruling was openly flouted by Hammond, who took it upon himself to fly to Cape Town while the others travelled the 1,000 miles by train, enduring in the process another timeless test of their patience[4].

There is one more burning question to consider: who would have won the match had it been played to a conclusion? As the game stood at that stage it was undoubtedly England's to lose (654 for five), though more likely than not the Kent cavaliers, Ames and Valentine, would have speedily acquired the 42 runs needed for victory. Verity, the next man in, had been good enough on one occasion to open the batting for England against Australia, and was more than capable of holding his own had he been called on; Wright, too, was no slouch. As a testimony of Verity's batsmanship there is none finer than Robertson-Glasgow's: 'He looks like Sutcliffe gone stale. That is, pretty good . . .' Yet in South Africa's favour the wicket was breaking up, albeit slowly, and their bowlers – drained to the core for the most part of Tuesday's play – had been re-energised by the late wickets of Paynter and Hammond. Who was to say that the game did not have one final twist to perform? After all, collapses had occurred from more advantageous positions before. As Duffus put it: 'It remains one of the eternal riddles of Test match cricket.'

Standing on the Kingsmead square 25 years later, the *Daily Telegraph* cricket writer Michael Melford remembered listening with fascination as Hammond and Melville, batting their theories back and forth, reflected on what might have happened had the timeless Test been allowed to run its true course. 'Each was absolutely convinced that he would have won,' he wrote. Even the arch-sceptic Pollock – who watched every ball and calculated that he had cabled some 10,000 words on 'the longest cricket serial ever thought of' – appeared to have been won over by the closing act:

> This timeless Test will go down in cricket history as the match there wasn't time to finish . . . And, by the cussedness of things, the game was just then in an intensely interesting state, threatening, at any moment, to keep developing sensationally, with the players suddenly keyed up, the spectators agog over the drama that might unfold before the final curtain . . . Then, just as the drama was nearly at its height, dark rain came teeming down, and the thrilled crowd saw no more. What a pity. What a match.

There was nothing left for the players to do after that but toast each other's health with copious champagne, and to conclude the series in the spirit and sportsmanship with which it had been conducted.

Hammond would later refer to the friendliness and good humour that existed between the two sides as 'unprecedented'. When the England team boarded the train for Cape Town that night they were sporting the green and gold ties of South Africa, while their opponents who had come to wave them off wore the dark blue, red and yellow of MCC. Among a roll-call of the English injured, Hutton and Gibb were both lame, and Edrich was nursing a sore shoulder. Nearly every player complained of a niggle or ailment of some kind or other, though it was nothing compared to the extreme fatigue felt by both teams; like the stragglers at a marathon, each man was utterly spent. Hammond, who had come to see his players off, was feeling his back; Melville was also lame, and Gordon and Langton – his lower back heavily strapped – had bowled themselves to a virtual standstill. No wonder that one newspaper carried the headline the next day, 'War of exhaustion'.

More champagne, no doubt, would help to dull the pain, and there were suggestions that several bottles had been smuggled on board by the England players. It would be a long night.

England: 316 & **654-5** (Edrich 219, Hammond 140, Gibb 120, Paynter 75, Hutton 55); **South Africa: 530** & **481**. Match drawn.

———

The following morning, Nourse decided to wander out to the middle and make a brief examination of the Kingsmead wicket. It was more out of curiosity than anything, though, as he said, 'There was no one to lay a wreath on the wicket after it was all over.' The crowds and the players had long gone, of course, but the sky was cloudless and the square, dappled in warm sunshine, looked in pristine condition. Once more the groundstaff had performed their conjuring tricks and, to his amazement, he discovered a wicket that would have 'rolled out better than ever had the necessity for its use arisen'. It was still rock-hard, he noted, 'dull and glazed, like a boxer who has received a knockout blow'.

Swanton also made a similar sortie out to the middle after the game was over and confirmed that 'the business end of the pitch was still flawless'. The only marks he detected were 'the shallow indentations behind the stumps made by the wicketkeepers'. It was almost as though 43 hours and 16 minutes of playing time, 1,981 runs and 5,447 balls had been mysteriously erased.

There is no doubt the 99th timeless Test deserved a decisive result, if only to reward the efforts of Verity, Gordon and Langton, who between them sent down 279 overs, straining every sinew and exhausting every weapon in their armoury, to exact a positive outcome from that pampered pitch. There is no doubt, too, the 22 players – not to mention the Kingsmead faithful – deserved better than the amateur theatrics and high farce that concluded the game. It was, as Duffus dubbed it, 'the father of all Test match freaks' – even if, in the end, it was only the wicket that remained timeless.

Seven
On Borrowed Time

'A new game has evolved. In the future reports will begin "so and so won the toss but it cannot be said they made full use of the first fortnight"' – Neville Cardus

England's departure from Cape Town on the afternoon of Friday, 17 March was an extravagant affair. Huge crowds lined the quayside, the sky seemed to fill with streamers, and a band played the *Athlone Castle* out into the smooth waters of Table Bay. There had been no more popular tourists than the strongest MCC side to tour South Africa, the first that could be said to have been truly representative of English cricket, and they received a send-off to remember. Record crowds followed them wherever they went, and in turn South Africa left its lasting impression on the players. Edrich was far from alone when in later years he recalled it as the happiest adventure of his cricketing life: 'I never remember a tour I liked better than the South African trip of 1938–39.' It was an appreciation amplified perhaps by the ever-present menace of war and what was likened to a 'final fling' attitude. Although anxious to return home each man, in his own way, was sad to be leaving this enchanted land behind.

Hutton, whose first MCC tour had exceeded all his expectations, told reporters he could not wait to come back; Perks said he would have been quite happy to stay another month; Verity – still proudly wearing the Springbok tie given to him by Bruce Mitchell – was considering an offer to return as a coach to Johannesburg; others, such as Wilkinson, were looking forward to two weeks' rest and relaxation on board. As they lined the main deck, casting their coins into Table Bay and making their silent pledges, some might even have wished never to see another timeless Test.

During the coming days and weeks the backlash against limitless cricket would be fast and furious, and was driven for the most part by the players themselves. Whether it was Hammond or Melville, Farnes or Gordon, Hutton or Nourse, both sides were unequivocal in their assessment: 'never again'. It was

Neville Cardus who observed of Hammond that he 'did not suffer boredom gladly', and the England captain made his feelings plain before the team sailed from Cape Town. 'I don't think timeless Test matches are in the best interests of the game, and I sincerely hope that the last one has been played,' he stated. Not even Ames, who was one of only two or three batsmen to stay loyal to their attacking instincts throughout, could find anything positive to say: 'We were naturally disappointed to be robbed of the opportunity of scoring the 42 runs required for victory, but by the end of the tenth day I am afraid few of us cared what happened.'

The whole weary process left Hutton convinced for the rest of his career that four days was ample time for a Test. Edrich, who benefited from the game more than most, agreed that it was 'an absurdity for any cricket match to go through ten playing days and two Sundays. There must be a time limit to matches'. In his autobiography, *Tours and Tests*, Farnes preferred not to dwell on it, pausing only to mention, 'As day followed day, and we trooped in and out of the pavilion, the whole performance became somewhat ludicrous. It was only raised from this by our amazing last innings, which far surpassed all records for a fourth-innings score.' A record that remains intact to this day.

The author Gerald Howat confirmed that for many of its participants the timeless Test became a way of life: Mitchell complained that 'it was like going to work every day', while Melville recounted that the groundsman telephoned him without fail at five o'clock each morning for his instructions, and that 'those five o'clock calls went on and on . . .' Melville was so exhausted that he was preparing to turn up at the ground on the last Sunday of the match only to be informed it was a rest day[1]. Dalton, though, had a more pressing concern: his wife grumbled that he woke her up most nights appealing for wickets in his sleep. By the end, Nourse admitted, 'Most of the joy had gone from it and we played merely because we were compelled to complete a contract we had started.'

There was a dissenting voice, however. Ronnie Grieveson, who emerged as one of South Africa's brightest talents and a natural heir to the great 'Jock' Cameron behind the stumps, simply did not want the match to end. Nor, of course, did the Kingsmead regulars who departed at the close of play every evening with the familiar and comforting refrain, 'See you tomorrow.' Perhaps there was a part of it that appealed, too, to the inner workings of the unconventional loner, Paul Gibb. Grieveson finished the series with a batting average of 57, completing seven catches and three stumpings – Hammond (twice) and Valentine – from only two appearances. His girlfriend became one of the Kingsmead regulars, watching every day of the Test, and he declared later he was so touched by her show of devotion that he married her shortly after.

———

Limitless cricket in England had been on borrowed time since before The Oval run-avalanche seven months earlier, and its demise was seen by many as being long overdue. By failing to fulfil its sole objective – namely to guarantee a positive result – 'this Durban monstrosity', as Cardus termed the timeless Test in the *Manchester Guardian*, had effectively sealed its own extinction. If there were any doubts, *Wisden* tightened the last screw on the coffin lid. 'The time limitless match we now believe to be dead,' it pronounced. The public outcry did the rest. In an age that embraced speed with a vigour and passion, and where the British racing ace Malcolm Campbell in *Bluebird* was smashing world records as the fastest man on both land and water, the timeless Test match had become a national embarrassment[2]. It was fodder for the music hall and radio comedians, and the headline writers and newspaper cartoonists had a field day at its expense.

Under the heading 'This Timeless Pest', one South African cartoonist exquisitely captured the mood, portraying an England batsman using his umbrella (a unique symbol of Englishness) as a bat, while his stumps were sent flying. Chamberlain was rarely seen in public without his rolled umbrella, and his many critics had seized on it as an emblem of his weakness. The caption read: 'When South Africa had dismissed Hutton, Hammond and Paynter it seemed that England's policy of appeasement would have to be abandoned.' Even 'The Cheeky Chappie' Max Miller, Britain's greatest stand-up comic of the era, managed to wring a few laughs out of the timeless Test amidst his customary rat-a-tat-tat of *double entendres*. But not everyone was laughing, as Jack Hobbs protested in his column in the *Star*: 'Timeless Tests must be stopped; cricket is not a joke.' His former opening partner, Herbert Sutcliffe, adopted a more subtle approach and, tapping unerringly into the general air of farce, could not resist the mischievous suggestion that, 'Perhaps in the next series of Tests, they should play one innings in England and the other in South Africa.'

Yet this was not even the first instance of a timeless Test failing to live up to its own definition – nor, for that matter, of a team having to scramble to catch the last boat home. The last Test of a four-match series between England and West Indies at Sabina Park,

Jamaica, in April 1930 (the teams were locked at 1–1) resulted in a similar fiasco. West Indies, set a staggering 836 to win, had reached 408 for five at the end of the seventh day, before the eighth and ninth were washed away by rain. England's ship sailed on the tenth day so that the players could return to their counties in time for the start of the new season, and the match was left unfinished. It yielded 1,815 runs and foreshadowed the plunder that was to come on the decade's run-drunk pitches. Surrey's Andy Sandham, at the age of 39, recorded Test cricket's first triple century – 325 – using a borrowed bat and boots. There was a gleaming double-hundred from the Jamaican George Headley – his 223 remains the highest score by a batsman in the fourth innings of a Test – while Ames, who had the unhappy distinction of playing in both aborted games, hit 149.

Further back in the mists of antiquity, the fate of two timeless Tests between England and Australia at Melbourne in 1882 was also decided by a steamship timetable. In the first, the ship due to take the England party to New Zealand was scheduled to leave on the morning of the fourth day, 4 January. The authorities put the departure time back to 3.45 p.m. in the hope that it would induce a positive result but Australia, chasing 382 to win, were still 155 runs shy with seven wickets in hand when the tie was abandoned as a draw. The final game of the four-match series in March went the same way after the England team had to depart to fulfil their final fixtures; as it was a private venture, the tour's coffers were their overriding priority. Once again the contest was left hanging in the balance on the fourth day.

Neville Cardus, having appointed himself as limitless cricket's critic-in-chief, continued to mock the concept unmercifully. 'A new game has evolved,' he announced in the wake of the Durban timeless Test. 'In the future reports will begin "so-and-so won the toss but it cannot be said they made full use of the first fortnight".' One county chairman even used the club's AGM to rail against what he called 'the blighting influence of timeless Tests', and feared the fad might catch on: 'Some batsmen might be persuaded to play as if they had a week to bat.' The South African authorities had already taken a lead by resolving that no more timeless Tests would be played on their soil. They advocated four-day Tests instead, which included two additional days put aside in case of rain or bad light. With draws considered the bugbear of international cricket, they moved that no wicket should be rolled once a Test was in progress.

Only the Australian Board of Control was convinced that timeless matches had a future, where they remained the hub of the country's cricket, and continued to push vigorously for all Ashes series in England also to be played to a finish. The matches at The Oval and Durban, it insisted, should be seen in the light of freak affairs and 'provided no valid argument for the abolition of timeless matches'. Australia's attachment to the limitless format was the immovable object against the irresistible force of change. 'In fairness,' Pollock reported, 'the Australians understand this highly specialised sort of cricket better than the English or South Africans.'

One Australian who had no qualms about contradicting his board, however, was the forthright Jack Fingleton. He called for an immediate ban on timeless Tests, predicting that, unless a time limit was imposed, the next series of Tests in Australia could also extend into ten days or beyond. Tellingly, he warned, 'Players do not look forward with any pleasure to Tests without a time limit, and the strain on them is tremendous.' In an unusual twist, another Australian journalist claimed later that The Oval and Durban 'freaks' were a conspiracy by Hammond and the England team 'to teach Australians the futility of long drawn-out matches'. The Englishmen, he continued, had 'purposefully spun out the game in Durban until the boat sailed . . . systematically ruining the Test and turning it into the greatest farce of all time'. If Hammond was guilty of anything, his biographer

Ronald Mason emphasised, it was that he did not possess 'among his techniques of captaincy any very effective plans for avoiding the impasse'.

Throughout it all Duffus remained the staunchest advocate for limitless cricket, especially the 'absorbing' Australian method of playing Tests to a finish, where pitches were consistently fast enough to sustain a positive attitude from both batsmen and bowlers. 'There is much to commend timeless Test matches,' he argued. 'The dullest cricket I have seen was in games of limited life, not magnificently drawn against time and odds but bereft of any hope of a decision by the end of the second day.' Although he acknowledged the Durban game had cheapened Test match values, it was not because it was timeless that it had done so: it was because of a wicket that was miraculously rejuvenated by rain on three separate occasions to 'live to an embarrassing old age'.

The preparation of wickets went to the heart of the matter. 'Bowlers could exercise every guile and still stand little chance of getting a normally careful batsman out in a week,' Hammond observed of most South African Test surfaces. During The Oval timeless Test Cardus had urged that, 'Something must be done to protect cricket from the constant danger of records being reared up and broken almost daily. An effort must be made to get back to the conditions when none but the greatest batsmen could hope to score a hundred in a Test-match innings.' In Swanton's opinion The Oval and Durban games were inextricably entwined. The pity for the latter, he explained, was that in following so closely behind the run-frenzy at The Oval it 'turned everyone decidedly away from timeless Tests. People blamed the lack of a limit instead of the root cause of the ennui, which in both cases was the pitch'.

R. C. Robertson-Glasgow, in *Wisden,* cited two chief reasons for the Durban débâcle: the 'undue solemnity of proceedings' and the imperishable pitch – it was 'plumb, but without pace . . . so far overstepping perfection as to be of little use to the bowler'. Yet the batsmen, he added, 'with few exceptions, cannot be wholly acquitted of blame. Some of them nearly slept on the pitch'.

There is little doubt that had the other batsmen followed the attacking blueprints of Ames and Valentine, or Dalton and Hutton for that matter, the frustration and farce could have been averted. The game threw up almost as many missed opportunities by batsmen on both sides to force the pace as it did Test records – an astonishing 23 of which were broken in all. South Africa's decision to stick with their safety-first tactics after tea on the sixth day, when Van der Bijl and Mitchell were entrenched at the wicket and

England's bowlers were all but out on their feet, was probably the most culpable. Hammond and Paynter too, on the final day, might have timed their onslaught a little sooner; after all, everyone knew the storm was coming. Nearly eight decades later, their reluctance to do so never fails to amaze.

For all that there was any number of heroic deeds to contemplate. Edrich's blazing double-century and emergence from the furnace of a dire run of low scores was the most heart-warming. 'I knew, of course, that the selectors would look askance at my record,' he wrote later, 'but I had justified myself to myself, and that was what mattered most of all.' Similarly, there was Van der Bijl's courage and conviction; the composed assurance of the batting artists, Hammond and Melville; the all-round excellence of Dalton; the rapid-fire stand by Ames and Valentine on the fourth day to rescue the game from an almost asphyxiating torpor. The 95.6 overs (766 balls) delivered by Verity should not be forgotten, nor the 92.2 overs (738 balls) from the tenacious Gordon and the 728 balls from Langton. If on the rare occasion Verity was forced to bowl 'like a book of instruction and give his soul a rest', as Robertson-Glasgow put it once, then who could blame him. Of course the 'deep tragedy', Duffus reflected, was that all those efforts were in the end to no avail, the countless runs and overs just 'so much energy fruitlessly squandered'. In their own way, no doubt, these were also records of a sort.

The wicket was another missed opportunity. It was too good to begin with and played better and better, with the assistance of rain, as the game progressed. In effect, Swanton wrote, the groundsman on each occasion 'made a new cake, which the tropical sun dried out before the start of play'. Ironically, had MCC consented to the South African proposal that the wickets be covered during the Test matches, the dry soil would in all likelihood have crumbled after four or five days, thereby allowing England to fulfil their last fixture against Western Province, and catch the boat home in their own good time – albeit perhaps with the series drawn 1–1.

The reform of over-prepared pitches became a matter of urgency after The Oval timeless Test, and the Advisory County Cricket Committee in England had already taken steps to ensure that the composition of wickets for the 1939 season did not 'unduly favour the batsmen'. Surrey would be at the forefront in their efforts to turn The Oval into the most competitive in the land. 'One of the justifiable criticisms against Test matches of unlimited time is that they encourage batsmen to play unnatural cricket,' Duffus pointed out. 'They can do that successfully only because they have confidence in the longevity of the pitches.' Regrettably, naturally gifted strokemakers such as

Nourse, Paynter and to a lesser extent Hammond fell into that trap in the earlier stages of the game in Durban and temporarily deserted their attacking principles. It would have been far better, Duffus concluded, to prepare a pitch that allowed bowlers to exploit their skills and batsmen to lose their wickets, rather than one on which 'both bowlers and batsmen should lose all character'. That was undoubtedly true, though ultimately it would not have saved timeless Tests from extinction. Their time had passed.

———

Hitler's patience had run out in Europe, too. At six o'clock on the morning of Wednesday, 15 March 1939, in dense snow, German troops marched into Prague. The invasion was all over in a matter of hours; aside from a few protestors who hurled snowballs at passing tanks, the full might of the German military machine met with no resistance. The Czechoslovakian army was swiftly disarmed and by the early afternoon huge swastikas illuminated buildings in the city and loudspeakers blared, 'Heil Hitler.' Czechoslovakia had fallen. Hitler entered Prague later that day, parading through half-deserted streets in an open-top Mercedes to an eerie silence. 'The Germans were installed as the undisputed masters of "golden"

Prague – without a single shot being fired,' one newspaper reported.

The first the England cricketers knew of the crisis was when they alighted at Cape Town in the early hours of Friday, 17 March, and saw the placards in the station. Their constant fear throughout the tour had been that war might break out at any moment while they were some 5,000 miles from home, and each man was desperate to devour the news, exhausted as they were by the long journey from Durban.

That same day, as the cricketers sailed from Cape Town for England, Chamberlain delivered a speech in his native Birmingham. His apathetic response in the House of Commons to Hitler's act of aggression and violation of the Munich Agreement had caused widespread anger. The policy of appeasement was in tatters; Britain had yet to lodge an official protest to Germany, and the silence of the prime minister was damning. On the train to Birmingham, however, he underwent a significant change of heart. He had planned to speak on domestic matters but, in an abrupt shift of tone and mood, he condemned Hitler for 'taking the law into his own hands'. In a speech broadcast to the nation, he asked solemnly, 'Is this the last attack upon a small state, or is it to be followed by others? Is this, in fact, a step in the direction of an attempt to dominate the world by force?' If that was the intention, he warned, 'No greater mistake could be made than to suppose that, because it believes war to be a senseless and cruel thing, this nation has so lost its fibre that it will not take part to the utmost of its power in resisting such a challenge if it ever were made.' The next day Britain informed Germany that the occupation of Czechoslovakia was 'a complete repudiation of the Munich Agreement . . . devoid of any basis of legality'. The countdown to war had begun.

'On the boat home we talked of little else but war,' Hammond admitted. 'Everyone knew that Hitler was poised to strike; no one could guess who the next victim would be, or whether the next cruel aggression would bring the world tumbling into chaos.' There had been the occasional sinister reminder, even in South Africa, of the impending conflict. As Hammond recalled, certain pro-German Afrikaners made no attempt to hide their hatred of Britain, or where their allegiances would lie in the event of a war: 'We had one or two glimpses of that rather vocal minority who still, at that time, understood Nazi principles so ill as to pretend to profess them.' Yet this was still the South Africa of coalition government, of Jan Smuts and J. B. M. Hertzog, united against the extreme nationalists. Smuts, once the sworn enemy of Britain but now a First World War hero, stalwart imperialist and architect of closer ties within the Commonwealth, entertained the England cricketers during their visit to Pretoria and told them he did not believe there would be another war. The German economy, he said, would be unable to withstand the strain. Edrich remembered they listened keenly to the soldier-statesman but that he and his team-mates had not shared his optimism[3].

The two-week voyage home also provided the players with ample time to reflect on what had been an unquestionably happy and successful venture. For Hammond – freed from the shadow of his *bête noire*, Bradman – his first tour as England captain was to all intents and purposes a triumph. He had presided over a contented crew and the harmonious team spirit, fostered aboard the *Athlone Castle* on the outward journey, sustained them for 161 days away from home. In later years he was much criticised for his lack of personal touch, and players were invariably left to fend for themselves. But as Howat pointed out, 'In those pre-war years the burden of responsibility touched him lightly.'

England took the series 1–0 – the first MCC team to win on South African soil for 16 years – were victorious in exactly half of their 18 games and remained unbeaten and largely injury-free throughout. Hammond's batting was supremely consistent, topping a thousand runs for the tour and averaging 87 in the Tests (609 runs), where he hit three centuries. According to his biographer Mason, he batted with 'an indolent controlled mastery that set him quite apart from any other batsman then playing except Bradman'. Duffus considered his batting to be 'still brilliant, but subdued' and added that he made 'an exemplary, resolute captain. He maintained firm control, set his field cleverly and was forever presenting batsmen with fresh strategies. His slip fielding was at times uncanny'. Swanton also praised Hammond at the time as a 'sagacious tactician' in *The Illustrated London News*, yet appeared 38 years later to have undergone a radical change of mind, claiming in his book, *Follow On*:

> As a captain he was defensive and quite lacking in flair and inspiration. He had an easy ride in South Africa in that his side never failed to make as many as were needed, while the bowling was always stronger and more varied than the opposition's, though similarly apt to be frustrated by the deadening ease of the pitches. Off the field he could be good company with those who amused him, cool and detached with those who did not. Seeing him at close quarters on this tour I felt he was the wrong man to lead England on future tours, while realising the difficulty in asking such a tremendous cricketer to step down . . .

Mason wrote that Hammond led England with his 'customary air of impassive and controlled detachment' and rated his captaincy as 'sensible but uninspired', though his promotion of Edrich in the second innings of the timeless Test in Durban had, he acknowledged, constituted an inspired moment.

The unqualified batting success of the tour, however, was the 37-year-old Paynter, who had several inspired moments – not least in the third Test at Kingsmead when he scored 243 to help set up the decisive victory of the series by an innings and 13 runs inside four days. It remained the highest Test score in South Africa for 31 years until superseded by Graeme Pollock's 274 against Australia, also at Kingsmead, in his country's last series before their expulsion from international cricket. Paynter's 653 Test runs at 81.62 was a record for a series aggregate in South Africa at that point; in all he scored 1,072 runs with five centuries.

After his world record 364 at The Oval, it was inevitable perhaps that Hutton would suffer a comparative dip in form, and he failed to complete an innings of three figures in the Tests, scoring 265 runs. Nonetheless, he saved his best for the provincial games and finished as the side's top-scorer overall with 1,168 runs at 64.88. He appeared to make a conscious effort after his marathon at The Oval to bat as attractively as he could at all times, as if determined to erase any suggestions that he was a stodgy player, and Duffus wrote that he performed with 'eager enterprise and daring recklessness to the surprise of the spectators'. *Wisden* went further and claimed that he 'looked the most accomplished player of the party'. Ames, with 339 Test runs at 67.80, Gibb (473 at 59.12) and Valentine (275 at 68.75) all seized their opportunities when they came, while Edrich (240) redeemed himself at the last. Ames was also a 'steady and sometimes brilliant wicketkeeper'.

On wickets so heavily loaded in favour of batsmen few bowlers on either side returned flattering figures, though Verity proved the least costly wicket-taker (19 in the series) at just over 29 apiece from 428 overs and was an unflagging model of accuracy. Farnes, with 16 wickets, was too often muzzled by the featherbed surfaces, but he roused himself magnificently in the third Test and was rewarded with match figures of seven for 109. Three of his four wickets in South Africa's second innings of the timeless Test were obtained during another archetypal spell of fast bowling.

Perhaps the unluckiest of the 15 English cricketers was the Sussex batsman Bartlett. The journalist and author David Foot recounts a story passed onto him by Swanton that might shed some light on why he was the one member of the party to miss out on Test selection. 'Bartlett was a magnificent player in 1938 and a very attractive chap,' Swanton recalled. In Bloemfontein, during MCC's game against Orange Free State, 'he made the cardinal error of showing a great deal of interest in the girl Hammond had his eye on. It was an unwise thing to do – to cross the captain like that'. Hammond was a married man and his philandering was hardly a closely guarded secret among the players and the press. Paynter, once asked about the merits of Hammond's captaincy, chose to ignore his more obvious qualities and responded instead with a typically blunt: 'Wally, well, yes – he liked a shag.' Bartlett had made an impressive start to the tour, hitting an unbeaten 91 against Western Province and taking a lavish century off Orange Free State in the self-same match, but his chances diminished afterwards, his form faded and he appeared in only 10 of the 18 fixtures.

At least his fortunes took a turn for the better on the voyage home. He and Yardley were reduced to their last few shillings by the time the team sailed from Cape Town; like the rest of their colleagues they had lived life to the full in South Africa. In one last defiant gesture they agreed to gamble their last ten shillings on the Grand National sweepstake and split the proceeds, if any. Much to their astonishment their horse – a rank outsider – romped home, earning the pair £50. They were so grateful at not having to return home penniless that they bought the organisers of the sweep three bottles of champagne from their winnings and still pocketed £23 each.

———

Once again South African cricket had punched way above its weight. In six years during the 1930s, before the arrival of Hammond's team, the Springboks participated in just two Test series: the victorious visit to England in 1935 and one against Australia shortly after, when they were found badly wanting against the twin-spin threat of Clarrie Grimmett and 'Tiger' O'Reilly. Cricket was almost exclusively the sport of the English stock and confined to the few English-speaking schools for recruiting purposes. As the Currie Cup went into cold storage during overseas tours, the selectors were restricted only to the provincial matches against MCC from which to gauge players' form and shuffle their limited resources.

It was difficult for the players to get the time off work, too, and Ken Viljoen joked that employers would be even more reluctant in light of the timeless Test. There remained, Swanton remarked, 'an inferiority complex at the heart of South African cricket that was not completely dissolved until the 1960s'. Farnes observed that their interest in the game could not compare with that of Australia: 'Rugby Union is undoubtedly South Africa's national game, and the Dutch element, which forms half of the white population, combines with the English in this.' The majority of Afrikaners had little appetite for playing or watching cricket at that stage, though Viljoen and Van der Bijl were notable exceptions. However, as Swanton wrote, he was joined in the box by an Afrikaans-speaking commentator for the latter part of the series. The word was spreading.

Despite its inherent problems, Duffus described the summer of 1938–39 as one of the most successful and productive in South African cricket. Melville had much to do with that, proving an astute and popular captain who grew in stature both as a batsman and a leader as the series progressed; he scored 286 runs – 248 of them in the last two Tests after wisely promoting himself to the top of the order. 'The virility of South African teams has always been refreshing,' Robertson-Glasgow noted in *Wisden*. And, as ever, they made full use of what talent there was at their disposal.

The advent of Norman Gordon as a Test bowler continued apace during the series and he finished as the leading wicket-taker on either side with 20 at 40.35. 'Without Gordon the attack might have fallen to a low level,' Duffus added. 'As it was, the bowlers did considerably better than was expected. However, South Africa lacks a fast bowler, a left-arm spinner and a slow bowler.' The single-minded Van der Bijl, another newcomer, played with a relentlessly straight bat to collect 460 runs at 51.11, while Mitchell (466 at 58.25) and Nourse (422 at 60.28) were nothing if not high-class. Dalton (220 runs and nine wickets with his leg-spin) was an enterprising all-rounder, and Langton rarely wasted the new ball, picking up 13 wickets with his variety of styles; Farnes considered him 'a trifle unlucky' as a bowler. His ability to chip in with useful runs down the order also served the Springboks well.

In addition, the financial returns from MCC's visit were prodigious and the overall effects were reported to have provided a 'wholesome and widespread stimulus' to the development of South African cricket. Yet it was not the only injection of cash the game received that summer. An unexpected windfall came about after a chance meeting between Swanton and the British car manufacturer and philanthropist, Lord Nuffield, who asked the journalist if there was any chance of a ticket for the third Test at Kingsmead. Swanton duly arranged it for Nuffield to watch the match from the players' balcony and he responded with an impromptu gesture, promising a donation of

£10,000 to South African cricket on the proviso that a suitable project could be submitted before he sailed in two days' time.

Hammond was invited to chair an *ad hoc* meeting with the South African Board of Control and the plan for an annual schoolboys' tournament – the Nuffield Schools Week, where many a future Springbok first came to prominence – was born[4]. One member of the board trumpeted it as 'the greatest thing to have ever been done for South African cricket'. Nuffield, in fact, liked the idea so much that he threw in another £500 for good measure before he went on his way. 'It was sad,' Swanton commented later, 'that no far-sighted person thought of bringing non-Europeans into the scheme. The fact is in the climate of that time it would not have occurred to anyone; but equally if it had done so there would have been no government objection.'

The fact of the matter was that racial segregation in South Africa, far from being relaxed during the 1920s and 1930s, had been hardened and consolidated, in sport as in all other areas of life. Swanton maintained, however, that he could recall no impressions of stark social injustice at the time. 'No doubt, I was young and heedless,' he concluded. The world that he and the England cricketers inhabited – the world of the travel brochure, luxury train compartments, deluxe hotels and glamorous social functions and parties – was a privileged one, and the South Africa they encountered and lovingly described in their various accounts would have appeared ostensibly untroubled and serene. It was the South Africa their hosts wanted them to see, just as the South African XI they wanted the world to see was a white one.

Rarely, in modern parlance, did the England players step out of their comfort zone. They tried their hand at surfing in Durban, played numerous rounds of golf and were regular guests at the races. They considered Newlands to be the most beautiful cricket ground in the world and the South African safari the most exciting and romantic of all the tours. In Johannesburg alone, Jack Holmes claimed, their popularity was such that they could have gone to three entertainments a night had they wished. 'The Australians told me that if I got the opportunity to go on the South Africa tour, I must go,' Farnes wrote. 'A very fine party, they said.'

Only Eddie Paynter, in his autobiography *Cricket All the Way*, felt the absence of the black player from the 'cricketing fraternity of South Africa' worthy of a mention, and his observations of the tour were written with the benefit of hindsight, 22 years later. 'Some of them do play cricket, but no matter how exceptional they become recognition is not granted to them in their own country,' he stated. The black South African could watch cricket from his segregated enclosure, and he might on occasion, if he was thought to be talented enough, bowl to white South Africans, Australians or Englishmen in the nets; but that was as far as it went. 'However good any black cricketer might be, he would not find selection for South Africa or any provincial side,' Howat recorded.

When George Mann brought the first post-war MCC side to South Africa in 1948–49, the black section of the crowd repeatedly made their voice heard by cheering every run and every wicket by the England team. The reason for this was not hard to fathom. Daniel F. Malan's National Party had just formed the first exclusively Afrikaner government and, with the enactment of apartheid, the country's future was taking an ominous and significantly more oppressive turn.

Eight
The Wrong End of a Telescope

*'Playing with one eye on the bowler and one on
the sky for raiding German bombers was
difficult' – Bill Edrich*

The *Athlone Castle* docked in Southampton on Friday,
31 March, after 14 leisurely days at sea. Yet again the
cricketers had managed to time their arrival to coincide
with the announcement of more bleak tidings. That
same day, in a ratcheting up of the stakes, Chamberlain
pledged to defend Poland – the most vulnerable of
Germany's neighbours and therefore Hitler's next
potential target – from any act of aggression. In such
an event, he stated: 'His Majesty's Government would
feel themselves bound at once to lend the Polish

Government all support in their power.' There could be no turning back now.

The cricketers caught the boat train to Waterloo where, after some cursory words from Hammond to the press (he praised his players for making the captain's job easy), they greeted their families, said their farewells to each other and went on their separate ways. Over the next few days they would report back to their counties for the start of the new season. No one was quite sure whether it would last two weeks or two months – all they knew was that it would be unlike any other they had played in.

On 26 April the government bowed to the inevitable and introduced conscription for men aged between 20 and 21, even though Chamberlain had vowed he would never do so in peacetime. Three days later, in the customary curtain-raiser to the season at The Parks and at Fenner's, Oxford University entertained Gloucestershire (minus their new captain, Hammond) and Cambridge played Northamptonshire. The eight-ball over was employed for the one and only time in an English cricket season, and slipped by almost unnoticed. The first round of championship matches followed seven days later and county cricketers went about their business again, not with the bright anticipation and optimism of seasons past, but out of a prevailing sense of duty. 'Day by day, we went out to amuse the public by our playing of a game, while loudspeaker vans toured the grounds crying for volunteers for the armed services,' Hammond recalled. Yardley complained that 'all first-class cricket seemed unreal and dreamlike. Such conditions made for erratic play; no one can concentrate on sport with war rumbling in the air'.

It was no different for those who reported on it. The droll Pollock started a diary in an effort to make some sense out of the general morass, but gave it up in the end ('It had too many libels in it, for one thing'). He had very few distinct memories of the 1939 season, he explained, other than that he knew war was coming any day: 'That conviction was always uppermost in my head, dulling all else.' His newspaper, the *Daily Express*, however, was still assuring its readers, even at this late hour, that there would be no war. Hutton remembered that, in the build-up to the season, 'it took us all our time to keep back the dread thought of approaching war'. Yet, playing at The Parks in early May, with 'the beautiful old trees as serene as ever' and the sun shining, he was suddenly overtaken by the notion that perhaps all his fears were exaggerated. 'Our minds see-sawed between hope and doubt,' he wrote.

West Indies toured England that summer, after an absence of six years, and brought a much-needed dusting of Caribbean magic to the sombre mood. The last time the countries met, in the winter of 1934–35, West Indies had claimed their first series triumph against England, 2–1; no one would be under-estimating them. The self-taught George Headley was a batsman to rival Bradman and Hammond, while Learie Constantine, at the age of 37, remained the most dexterously gifted all-rounder in the world: a wonderfully inventive, unorthodox batsman and a dangerous fast bowler, who cunningly adapted his pace as he grew older and could turn his hand to wrist or finger-spin. He was probably the greatest fielder the game has known – the Australians nicknamed him 'Electric Heels' – and he captivated crowds wherever he played. 'Anyone who ever watched him will recall with delight his particular parlour trick,' *Wisden* wrote. 'When a ball from him was played into the field, he would turn and walk back towards his mark: the fieldsman would throw the ball at his back, "Connie" would keep walking and, without appearing to look, turn his arm and catch the ball between his shoulder blades. No one, so far as can be ascertained, ever saw him miss.'[1]

The weather was bitterly cold during the early weeks of the season and a snow storm interrupted a West Indies' practice session, shortly after their arrival. 'The snow amazed one or two members of the side, who had never seen it before,' Hammond wrote. Not surprisingly they made an indifferent start, losing heavily in their first game against Worcestershire, where it was a battle just to stay warm, let alone keep a rampaging Reg Perks at bay; the England fast bowler returned match figures of 11 for 75. Further defeats quickly followed against Surrey and Glamorgan. However, the visitors perked up as the temperatures rose and, after a resounding victory over Middlesex by an innings and 228 runs, went into the first Test at Lord's in late June with their confidence restored and with Headley and Constantine – the latter having performed handstands in the field against Middlesex to the delight of the spectators – in exultant form.

There were only five survivors from the timeless Test (Hammond, Hutton, Paynter, Verity and Wright) when the England selectors announced their team for Lord's. The most conspicuous omission was undoubtedly that of Edrich. As *Wisden* commented: 'There can surely be no parallel for a batsman failing in eight consecutive Tests and yet keeping his place, but one would expect that, when he had at last justified the selectors' confidence, he would have retained it.' Like all cricketers during the summer of 1939 Edrich felt its untold pressures – 'Playing with one eye on the bowler and one on the sky for raiding German bombers was difficult' – but he still managed to hit seven championship centuries, averaging close to 50, and 'play some of the best cricket of his life'. Hardly surprising, either, that in such a vein of form he confessed to feeling as if he was somehow invisible to the selectors.

His biographer, Alan Hill, suggests that, 'despite his revival, he was required to serve a season of penance', though he does not elaborate further. As it transpired, of course, it would prove to be far longer than that. Writing in his autobiography *Cricket Heritage*, nine years later, Edrich concluded, 'My final big score in South Africa had not been impressive enough alone, and plenty of runs in county games did not wipe out the accusation that had been so freely levelled that I had not got Test match temperament.' Within a few months he would demonstrate that those accusations could not have been wider of the mark. Whatever Edrich may have lacked as a cricketer or a man, it was most certainly not temperament, nor nerve for that matter.

Ames was also missing from the team, but his absence was more straightforward. In May, after being advised by his doctor that his back would not stand the strain of keeping wicket on a regular basis, he took the decision to put away the gloves and concentrate exclusively on his batting. 'By that time it was becoming pretty hard work to combine the two jobs,' he admitted. Gibb might have been the selectors' first choice to take over behind the stumps had he not chosen to take a year off. Farnes's appearances were limited by his teaching commitments and responsibilities as a housemaster at Worksop College, and he played only eight first-class games that summer. Valentine, meanwhile, continued to flourish as one of the most attractive batsmen on the circuit, yet seemed destined to never play a Test in England.

The Test matches were allotted only three days and Hammond, despite his strong resistance to long drawn-out cricket, did not approve. 'It is almost impossible to finish a game between international teams in three days,' he insisted (he might have added that it could not always be done in ten days either), 'and the tendency of the victor is to then play for a draw once a Test has been won. This undoubtedly spoils cricket.'

Nonetheless, some 55,000 people passed through the turnstiles at Lord's, the Test generated four centuries and any number of scintillating strokes, before England wrapped it up by eight wickets with 35 minutes to spare on the final day. Despite the tourists' defeat, the game was a personal triumph for Headley: the batsman, dubbed 'The Black Bradman', scored a century in each innings to repeat the trick he performed against England at Georgetown in

1930. His legion of faithful admirers back home in Jamaica conversely referred to Bradman as 'The White Headley' – a clever juxtaposition and one that, in the view of *Wisden*, amounted to a pardonable exaggeration. Hutton, though, marvelled at much of Headley's strokemaking and revealed that he had never seen a batsman play the ball so late (not even Bradman) nor with such freedom. Denis Compton, having wintered with Arsenal, hit 120 on his return to Test cricket and put on 248 for the fourth wicket with Hutton, who scored 196 just three days after celebrating his 23rd birthday.

The weather was miserable throughout and, for the second time in three months, England found themselves concluding a Test match to the ominous rumble and crackle of thunder – a sound that, on this occasion, was heavy with symbolism. The threat of encroaching war was impossible to avoid. The slogan 'National Service – have you offered yours?' confronted crowds on the hoardings as they made their way to Lord's; inside the ground they were faced with the variation, 'National Service – are you playing?' Hammond was called on during the Test to make several appeals for men to volunteer; on other occasions, music rang out over the loudspeakers for the crowd's entertainment – the first time anyone could remember that happening at Lord's. It was far from normal service.

The weather turned decidedly sour again for the second Test in Manchester over 22–25 July and cheerless temperatures, rain and bad light, unforgiving even by Old Trafford's standards, reduced play to barely two full days. 'Only heroes would come to Old Trafford in an English summer,' Hammond remarked. And plenty of them did, as it turned out. The England captain had to make more appeals for volunteers, this time from an RAF van inside the ground, recruiting, in his own words, 'young men against the dark future'. Inevitably the game fizzled out in a predictable draw. Yet, despite the paucity of cricket, the public's hunger for the game remained ravenous and as many as 28,000 showed up during the three days, including 11,000 on the Saturday who waited patiently in the cold and rain when only 64 balls were bowled.

During August Farnes returned for Essex in the County Championship, and a compelling case could have been made for his inclusion in the final Test of the summer at The Oval. He had kept himself extremely fit during the school term, bowling in the nets whenever the opportunity arose. He also appeared for the Gentlemen against the Players at Lord's in July. An elemental force of nature at his best, this was a fixture that rarely failed to stir his blood. He was distinctly quick in the Players' first innings, ripping out three batsmen in just six balls to capture five for

78 from 19 overs. In seven games for his county he picked up a further 33 wickets, including five in an innings on three occasions, and completed a hat-trick – the only one of his first-class career – against Nottinghamshire in the penultimate round of championship matches before the start of the Second World War. Raw pace, as Robertson-Glasgow reaffirmed in *Wisden*, was a priceless commodity, and in his 'Notes on the 1939 Season' he lamented the fact there was not a bowler in English cricket 'to cause the wicketkeeper's gloves to go off like a paper bag, or the spectators to suck in the long-drawn breath'. He added that, 'There was one, 'K. Farnes, of Essex. But he was a full-time schoolmaster, and had betaken his art at half-pace to the practice nets.'

Farnes's late burst of form did not propel him back into the England team, and Worcestershire's Perks was summoned to The Oval instead. Once again the in-form Edrich and Ames – the latter scored the fastest century of the season against Surrey in 67 minutes – had failed to sway the selectors. More surprisingly, Paynter and Verity, the batting and bowling mainstays in South Africa, were left out. The MCC party to tour India that winter had already been named, though no one expected them to travel. It was not even remotely close to full-strength, and therefore hardly representative. Hammond, Yardley and Valentine among others had declined invitations, and Jack Holmes, England's manager in South Africa, would captain a side that included Hugh Bartlett.

The Oval might easily have passed for a fortress when the third Test got under way on Saturday, 19 August. There were barrage balloons overhead – 'silvery shapes of cruel omen', as Constantine graphically described them – and an anti-aircraft gun mounted on a tractor. The players learned that the weapon was kept permanently on the move to deceive German spies into mistaking the city's four guns for a greater battery. The Oval would later be requisitioned and adapted as a prisoner-of-war camp. The author Derek Birley pointed out that, according to some, its architectural style rendered it a natural choice for the role. During the game Constantine recollected seeing 'hard and frightened faces; there was the drone of flying to be heard, unusual then in London; khaki and naval blue and a sprinkling of Air Force uniforms showed everywhere among the crowds'. But there was also glorious sunshine for once, and the runs gushed: 1,216 over three days. Hammond struck 138, his 22nd Test century to eclipse Bradman's number, and Hutton ended the game with an undefeated 165, giving further notice of his 'ripening greatness', almost a year to the day since his world-record 364 against Australia at the same ground.

The highlight of the West Indies batting was a shimmering 79 from Constantine, an innings that had all the fanfare of a grand and final fling. The Trinidadian clattered 11 fours and a six off 92 balls from an attack that sadly lacked Verity's guile and control. So spectacular was his hitting that at one point Hammond stationed nine men on the boundary, but still failed to stem the onslaught. *Wisden*, in particular, waxed lyrical: 'He revolutionised all the recognised features of cricket and, surpassing Bradman in his amazing strokeplay, he was absolutely impudent. With an astonishing stroke off the back foot Constantine thumped Perks for six to the Vauxhall end – a very long carry. Seldom can there have been such a spread-eagled field with no slips . . .' He was dismissed, attempting another soaring six off Perks; the ball climbed so high, Hammond recalled, that the wicketkeeper Arthur Wood, having tracked its trajectory all the way from his position behind the stumps, ended up almost catching it in the pavilion.

After trailing West Indies by 146 runs on the first innings, England easily played out a draw, reaching 366 for three to claim a series victory in the process. Hammond and Hutton put on 264 for the third wicket at 80 runs an hour, as if to give the crowd something golden to cherish before the curtain came down on Test cricket for seven years, and the lights went out.

'Everyone knew the war was only weeks, or days, away,' Hammond wrote. It was heady batting, and a crowd of almost 10,000 left The Oval yearning for more.

It was not to be. The following day, 23 August, Germany and Russia signed a non-aggression pact, in which the two countries agreed to undertake no military action against each other. The news landed with the shocking force of a bombshell, and left the door open for German troops to march into Poland unopposed. With the noose tightening around Warsaw and events unravelling at terrifying speed across Europe, the pragmatic decision was taken to cancel the remaining four matches of the West Indies tour. Four days later the party sailed from Greenock for Montreal on the SS *Montrose*, declining Sussex's plea to play their match and 'keep the flag flying'; the two teams were scheduled to meet at Hove over three days, starting on 26 August. The waters were already infested with U-boats, and Howat makes the point that had West Indies relented they might have boarded the next ship, the SS *Athenia*, which was torpedoed in the Atlantic without warning on 3 September[2].

———

Sussex and Yorkshire contested the last County Championship game of the 1939 season at Hove on

30 August–1 September. The stumps had been pulled early in the two remaining fixtures between Lancashire and Surrey at The Oval, and Leicestershire and Derbyshire at Aylestone Road, Leicester, but at Hove the decision was taken to play on. The championship had maintained its hold on the public until the end and, despite the anticipation of war, there was no shortage of vigorous cricket or individual fulfilment.

In his retrospective on the season, written during the first few months of the war, Robertson-Glasgow concluded that many had turned to cricket as they would an old friend, one 'who gives you a seat, a glass of beer, and something sane to talk about'. But the time for sanity was long passed, and the season had already acquired the glow of nostalgia; to look back on it was like 'peeping curiously through the wrong end of a telescope at a very small but very happy world', Robertson-Glasgow ventured. 'It is a short six months since Constantine gave the England bowlers such a cracking at The Oval, like a strong man suddenly gone mad at fielding practice, but it might be six years, or sixteen; for we have jumped a dimension or two since then in both time and space.'

The denouement at Hove is remembered above all things for the bowling of Verity, whose figures of seven for nine from 48 balls delivered Yorkshire their 20th championship victory of the season, by nine wickets. Sussex had capitulated in their second innings for only 33 in the space of 11.3 overs. Their batsmen can be forgiven for having their minds on other matters, though that is not to take anything away from Verity: as ever he was immaculacy itself and obtained considerable turn from a wicket that was breaking up under a blazing sun. Yet he did not appear to derive any great satisfaction from his performance. Indeed, Alan Hill writes that he was 'unusually subdued, not even offering the characteristic twinkle of a smile at his latest conquest'. Afterwards he could only wonder quietly 'if I shall ever bowl here again'. Having predicted that war would come, and last for six years, his touching expression of doubt seemed almost to carry the weight of premonition.

Verity had arrived at the end of a remarkable run of form: against Kent at Dover, a week earlier, he captured match figures of nine for 80, and a few days later produced another significant haul, seven for 51, to rout Hampshire in Bournemouth. His nine for 117 during the Brighton and Hove Cricket Week took his tally of wickets for the season to 191 at 13.13 off 936 overs, and put him far and away at the head of the first-class bowling averages for the second time in his career. In the words of J. M. Kilburn, the polished correspondent of the *Yorkshire Post*, it was, despite the strident noises off, 'cricket of uncommon quality'.

Yorkshire had already sewn up their seventh championship title of the decade by the time they played Sussex, and their visit to Hove was no more than a simple case of applying the trimmings. Middlesex had kept them honest throughout, finishing as deserving runners-up, while Gloucestershire and Essex were third and fourth respectively. Hammond, in his first season as county captain, topped the first-class batting averages for the seventh successive year (2,479 runs at 63), just ahead of Hutton (2,883 at 62), and his leadership was singled out by *Wisden* for 'setting a fashion in enterprising cricket and a spirit of adventure which made Gloucestershire second to none as an attraction'. In the summer of 1939, Edrich recalled, 'the counties fought as hard and doggedly as ever, but feverishly. Cricketers are used to playing with one eye on the clock – but, that season, we were watching the remorseless hands of a bigger clock move towards the hour of destiny, and we knew it.' That hour had already struck and, when Yorkshire's Wilf Barber hit the winning runs at Hove on the afternoon of 1 September, German bombs were falling on Warsaw and the invasion of Poland had begun.

Understandably the spectators were reluctant to leave at the end of the game and, instead of drifting slowly home with their thoughts as they would normally have done, found any excuse to linger and talk. During the day's play they had applauded politely though not wholeheartedly, as if they were watching yet not watching. In the pavilion, among the rows of deck chairs or around parked cars, where there was the constant crackle of wirelesses, war was the all-consuming topic and the figures on the field appeared almost ghostlike. 'Lots of spectators bought scorecards as mementoes, probably thinking that this was the last cricket they would ever see,' Hutton observed. 'Friends crowded into the pavilion and both dressing-rooms to say goodbye.' The journalist Pollock was among them. 'Len Hutton, champion batsman of the year, was looking very pale and serious,' he noted. 'He won't get his 3,000 runs for the season now.'

Not long after, the Yorkshire players left the ground by coach on the start of their long journey back to Leeds, stopping only briefly at Leicester *en route* to snatch an hour or two's fitful sleep in a pub lounge. 'The further we got from Brighton, and the more we saw and heard of England on the eve of war – already there were evacuee children, and searchlights, and a blackout in every town and village we rode through – the deeper was our conviction that we would be lucky if we ever played cricket again,' Hutton remembered.

That same night, two days before Britain declared war on Germany, Pollock jotted in his diary, 'The start to evacuate three million people, mostly children, has begun and kids with labels stuck on them and bits of luggage in their hands have poured into Brighton. On the *Star* billboard I saw for the first time the word "Evacuees".' His final entry was suitably stark: 'Brighton is blacked out tonight . . .'

And time had never felt so precious.

Epilogue
The Timeless Men

Timeless Test matches were never officially abolished after 1939 – instead, they were left to wither on the vine and simply fade away. In truth, the administrators didn't need to do anything: the titanic failure of the Durban timeless Test to produce a result had done it for them and ensured there would be no repeat. 'The impression it made was so deep that there has never been another since,' Swanton wrote. To a certain extent the concept was also overtaken by events and, when first-class cricket resumed after a gap of seven years in 1946, the world had changed irrevocably. Timeless Tests were already the unlamented relic of another age.

Indeed, the emergence of the fledgling one-day game during the war years proved such an unqualified success with the public that it opened up a whole new world of

227

possibilities. One-day cricket was staged regularly at Lord's on Saturdays and, because it provided the instant gratification of a result, especially at a time of war, became hugely popular. Its lionisation even prompted Hammond to wonder whether the game would not need to adopt 'new forms and revolutionary changes' if it was to preserve its popularity: 'It has been suggested that three-day matches would make too great a demand on the time of spectators in this world of rush and hurry.' Surprisingly, the public would have to wait until 1963 before a one-day knockout competition, the Gillette Cup, was finally introduced to English cricket.

Bradman also concerned himself with the future of the game, and in an article in the 1939 edition of *Wisden* – 'Cricket at the crossroads' – he urged the administrators to adapt to the quickening tempo of the world, adding that, 'We cannot arrest nor impede the tenor of everyday life whether in business or sport.' He cited the Leeds Test of 1938, where Australia retained the Ashes, as the shining exemplar for modern Test cricket:

> The match was one succession of thrills. People fought to get into the ground, not out of it. Their hearts beat frantically with excitement, mine along with the rest of them. Did anyone think of that curse of modern cricket – batting averages? No! It was the game which mattered. Australia won. She

nearly lost and if she had it would have been a greater game still. It was stirring, exhilarating cricket. There wasn't even time to think of timeless Tests at Leeds.

Australia duly took note, and the 1946–47 Ashes series was the first to be staged in Australia where Tests were not played to a finish. The matches were of six days' duration, though it seemed Australia could not give up the format completely, after it was agreed that the fifth Test would be timeless if neither side led the rubber by more than one. As it transpired, it was not needed and trial by timeless Test was avoided. Australia's system for limitless cricket, it should be pointed out, had served them perfectly well for 62 years, where the climate and the hard wickets invariably encouraged positive play and a decisive result. 'They are tough out there,' Hammond recalled, 'and do not like no-decision fights.' In fact, the two drawn Tests of the 1946–47 series were the first of their kind to be played in Australia since 1882.

Timeless Tests in Australia and England had always been two very different beasts. In England, they were usually regarded with a mixture of suspicion and loathing – to the extent that one critic, the wife of the author and former cricketer Robert Lyttelton, condemned them for their 'stodginess' and what she called 'suet-pudding tactics' after England had been roundly defeated by Australia in the 1930 timeless Test at The Oval. But even worse, she had commented in the *Sunday Times*, was 'the severe attack of sciatica brought about by timeless sitting'.

———

The Durban timeless Test of 1939 was the final gasp of a cricketing epoch, a sparkle of innocence and glamour that disappeared for ever. It also represented the last international appearance of nine of its participants, six South Africans – Van der Bijl, Dalton, Grieveson, Langton, Newson, Gordon – and three Englishmen: Ames, Valentine and Farnes. At least six of them had to accept that their Test days were over after losing six years of their cricketing lives to the war, while another was too badly wounded to continue his; but Farnes and Langton were not so fortunate. Both men died on active service within a year of each other. Pilot Officer Farnes was the third English Test player to lose his life in the conflict, on 20 October 1941, after Geoffrey Legge (Kent) and George Macaulay (Yorkshire), and only the fourth international cricketer to do so. Flight Lieutenant Langton died on 27 November 1942 and was the second South African fatality after the batsman 'Dooley' Briscoe, who won the last of his two caps against Hammond's team in the second Test at Newlands on 31 December 1938.

Verity, who played his final Test for England against West Indies at Lord's in June 1939, was the eighth out of nine international cricketers from around the world to make the supreme sacrifice, and the third from the timeless Test. A fervent patriot and proud Yorkshireman, Captain Verity of the Green Howards believed utterly in the cause for which he gave his life on 31 July 1943. Farnes and Verity, of course, could justifiably lay claim to being the two finest bowlers of their type available to the England selectors in the period just before the Second World War. The all-rounder Langton had been an integral part of the South African side since his debut in 1935, when he came to England as the youngest member of Herbert Wade's popular and triumphant 15-man party and endeared himself to the crowds. In the assessment of Robertson-Glasgow, he was a 'resourceful and artistic bowler'.

Sergeant Observer Ross Gregory, of the RAAF, became the first Australian Test cricketer to be killed in action, on 10 June 1942, and there is a haunting and enduring poignancy attached to his death: he played his last Test against England at Melbourne in February 1937 when he was dismissed 20 short of his maiden century – caught Verity, bowled Farnes. David Frith, the cricket historian and author, wrote that there is 'no parallel in Test history in terms of future tragedy'.

THE FALLEN

Kenneth Farnes (1911–41)

Cambridge University and Essex

Record in the timeless Test: bowled 68.1 overs for five wickets, including second-innings figures of four for 74. Scored 20 runs in England's first innings.

Farnes died on his first unsupervised night-flying exercise at RAF Chipping Warden, in Northamptonshire, when his Wellington bomber crashed in the village after he attempted to abandon his landing. He was just a week away from becoming operational. Farnes had been based at Chipping Warden for only a month after earning his wings in Medicine Hat, Alberta, Canada, where he passed out top of his group. He would have chosen to fly Spitfires had he had his way but was unable to squeeze his 6 foot 5 inch frame into the cockpit, so he volunteered instead for night flying. According to David Thurlow, the author of *Ken Farnes: Diary of an Essex Master*, he was killed on impact and his co-pilot died later in hospital: 'He managed to avoid most of the houses, hitting the ground in a tennis court and coming to rest in a garden at Hogg End. The crash set the roofs of some thatched houses on fire but no villager, incredibly, was killed. It was appalling for the woman he loved because she was waiting at the airfield for him . . . Within moments of the disaster she knew.' Thurlow explained that Farnes 'wanted to be a flyer, not a gunner nor the man who pressed the button to release the bombs because he told his family he could not do that, not drop a bomb on someone hundreds of feet below whom he did not know nor see'. A commemorative plaque, unveiled at Chipping Warden in November 2013, marks the spot where he died, aged 30.

Farnes took 60 wickets in 15 Tests at 28.65 and achieved his best haul of six for 96 against Australia during the fifth Test at Melbourne in 1937. He also returned match figures of ten for 179 on his Test debut against Australia at Nottingham three years earlier, one of only six Englishmen to have achieved the feat. It was not, however, enough to prevent England from suffering a 238-run defeat. In an article for *Boy's Own Paper* in August 1939, Farnes vividly described what it was like to bowl to Bradman on his England debut, though modesty precluded him from mentioning either the ten wickets or his dismissal of Bradman for 25 in the second innings: Bradman merely 'made low scores in each innings of the Test'. Farnes was never tempted to write about the timeless Test, and certainly not in *Boy's Own*, whose readers might have dismissed it as too far-fetched even for their tastes. His fellow pace bowler, the Yorkshireman Bill Bowes, tells an affecting little tale about him. The young freshman was playing for Essex against Yorkshire at Scarborough in 1932 and had the misfortune to run into the England batsmen Herbert Sutcliffe and Maurice Leyland on a flat track, in the form of their lives. Farnes bowled four overs for 75 runs, and the faster he bowled the further they hit him. After the game, Bowes discovered him in tears. 'I'll never make a fast bowler,' Farnes said. Bowes told him it was a matter of experience, that's all.

And so it was. In all first-class cricket Farnes captured 690 wickets at 21.45 in 168 games, despite the fact that the surfaces of the era often sapped his venom. He had few pretensions as a batsman but once hit 97 against Somerset at Taunton in two hours; his failure to convert it into a century elicited only laughter from him on this occasion. He would have undoubtedly played more Tests for England had his commitments as a teacher and housemaster at Worksop College not taken precedence. In a moving tribute to Farnes, the headmaster of Worksop College, the Reverend B. C. Maloney, wrote in *The Times*:

> The news of his death has come as a great shock to all who knew him at Worksop. To the majority of his countrymen the news has come of the loss of

one of the greatest fast bowlers; to masters and boys at this school it means the loss of a valued friend and counsellor. Farnes was an energetic and untiring teacher of history and geography and an able and much-loved housemaster. To this latter position he was appointed at an unusually young age and his success therein was largely due to the quite natural modesty of the man, which made him as willing to learn from boys as they were from him. A giant in stature, he had the greatness of voice and manner which so often accompanies great size and strength and, though on the cricket field he would rouse himself to devastating action, he never let his strength run away with him.

He invariably reserved his most potent performances for the Gentlemen versus Players fixture at Lord's. One such occasion was the game in 1938 when his eight for 43 in the Players' first innings was considered by Swanton to be the most ferocious spell of fast bowling he had seen in England. 'Larwood was fast in 1930, Lindwall and Miller in 1948, Hall and Griffith in 1963, and at their peak all these were probably faster than Farnes. But he could be roused by an occasion to a different degree of speed,' he wrote. Jack Fingleton, who faced him on numerous occasions, also admired the rugged fury of his pace and celebrated him as the 'most handsome Test cricketer of his age, a movie star in looks, but better than his looks was his modest, cheerful and cultured company'. Had he survived the war he would have been about to turn 35 when cricket resumed again, and in all likelihood his fastest days were behind him. However, his autobiography, *Tours and Tests*, provides an intriguing insight into an engaging, erudite man and the game of that time, and he would have had much still to give the sport, later perhaps as a writer, a vocation for which he nurtured serious ambitions. Sadly, the warehouse stock of *Tours and Tests*, published in 1940, a year before his death, was destroyed in a bombing raid and has since become something of a rarity.

Arthur Chudleigh Beaumont Langton (1912–42)

Transvaal

Record in the timeless Test: bowled 91 overs for four wickets,
including first-innings figures of three for 71. Scored
33 runs in two innings, and held one catch.

The red-haired 'Chud' Langton came to prominence as an all-rounder of note at Lord's in 1935 when, with match figures of six for 89 and an invaluable second-innings knock of 44, he helped South Africa complete their first Test victory in England. In the words of *Wisden*, the 23-year-old was 'the big discovery of the tour', claiming 15 wickets in five Tests and boasting a batting average of 30.25. A versatile right-arm bowler, he could switch between fast-medium, medium, or spin, depending on the conditions. In his faster style he made the most of his 6 feet 3 inches to telling effect, obtaining awkward lift while swinging the ball appreciably. His batting was at its best when he went after the ball, as he did at The Oval in the final Test of 1935, stroking his highest score – an undefeated 73 – in a ninth-wicket stand of 119 in 137 minutes with Eric Dalton, cutting, pulling and driving the England bowlers to his heart's content.

His record in the 1938–39 series, when he captured 13 wickets at 51.69 and scored only 115 runs, did not suggest great things, but England always remained wary of his all-round ability. Invariably, he was the first bowler Melville threw the ball to and retained his captain's faith throughout the series. He produced his best figures in the fourth Test at Johannesburg, returning five for 58 on a rare occasion when the conditions favoured the bowlers. But, after making an aggressive 64 in the first Test – he was an imposter coming in as low as No. 10 in the order – his batting tailed away. He played with a strapped back during England's second innings in the timeless Test, yet still managed to flog his way through 56 overs, delivering 91 in all, placing him fifth on the all-time list for the most balls bowled in a Test (728). Only Verity and Gordon exceeded that number in the match.

He enlisted in the South African Air Force during the war and achieved the rank of Flight Lieutenant. He died when his Lockheed B-34 Ventura bomber spun and crashed on landing at Maiduguri in Nigeria. His death, at the age of 30, was deeply mourned in South Africa and Dudley Nourse recalled him as a 'lion-hearted bowler'. He would almost certainly have returned to England in 1947 when the Springboks undertook their first post-war tour. His 15 Tests brought him 40 wickets at 45.67 and he scored 298 runs at 15.68.

Hedley Verity (1905–43)

Yorkshire

Record in the timeless Test: bowled 95.6 overs for four wickets, and scored three runs in England's first innings.

News of Verity's death broke on 1 September 1943, exactly four years to the day that he took seven Sussex wickets for nine runs at Hove in the last match of the 1939 season and had wondered aloud whether he would ever play there again. Two days later the War Office and the Red Cross confirmed that Captain Verity, a prisoner of war, had died of his wounds in an Italian military hospital in Caserta on 31 July. In the all-conquering Yorkshire side of the 1930s, blessed with an apparently limitless seam of extraordinary cricketers and characters (Hutton, Sutcliffe, Leyland, Bowes, Yardley, Wood), it would be no exaggeration to say, as many did, that Verity was the greatest and the best loved of all.

He joined the Green Howards, more frequently known as the Yorkshire Regiment, in 1939 and was soon posted to the 1st Battalion. He served in Northern Ireland, India and Egypt – where, in the words of another Green Howard, Yardley, he helped himself to his 'usual bag of wickets' at Cairo's Gezira Sporting Club – before the regiment landed in Sicily for the allied assault on Catania in July 1943. B Company, led by Captain Verity, launched the Green Howards' offensive against the German positions in the early hours of 20 July, supported by a barrage of artillery fire. Verity commanded around one hundred men and was experiencing his first taste of combat. Doubtless the responsibility weighed deeply on him but he was already a highly regarded officer, having applied the same analytical brain and tactical acumen of the cricketer to his soldiering. The onslaught on Catania, however, would test him in ways that he could never have foreseen.

Initially, B Company had to stay dug in for an hour while the artillery shells screamed overhead. When the big guns fell silent, they advanced for at least half a mile in moonlight across ditches and water courses towards the German positions, before entering a cornfield. There they ran into a torrential hail of tracer bullets and mortar fire. Soon it was coming at them from all angles; the trees and corn had started to burn, too, leaving them trapped and exposed. Surrounded on all sides, Verity was left with no option but to urge his men forward. He had remained steely and calm under the withering fire, staying at the head of his company, but realised he needed to act swiftly and decisively if they were to survive. The strong point appeared to be a farm building to their left. Verity gave the order for one platoon to attack the position and another to provide covering fire. Moments later he was hit in the chest by flying shrapnel but, still leading his men, shouted, 'Keep going. Get them out of the farmhouse and me into it.'

Verity's loyal batman, Private Tom Rennoldson, stayed with him after he fell, while the remainder of the company continued to advance. The two had formed an inseparable bond after serving together in Ireland, India and Egypt. Rennoldson, a Geordie, used to joke that he'd never watched a game of first-class cricket: 'I used to say to the captain that I couldn't understand how anyone who bowled 'em so slow as he did could get anyone out. He would laugh and say that some day he would show me.' By 4.30 a.m. the battle was over and the remnants of B Company had retreated, leaving Verity and Rennoldson stranded behind enemy lines. Later that morning the Germans came and the pair were captured. Verity was put on to a broken mortar carrier, packed with sheaves of corn, and carried to a field hospital, where he underwent an emergency operation. As they lifted Verity on to the operating table, a grenade rolled out of his shirt pocket and there was a moment of panic before Rennoldson calmly unprimed it. After the operation Rennoldson was taken away and transported to a POW camp in Austria; he never saw his captain again.

Verity and the rest of the wounded prisoners were ferried by open railway trucks through Sicily and put on board a ship to Reggio in southern Italy. He spent a night in a military hospital before being moved by goods train to Naples – a journey that lasted almost two excruciating days, with little food or water – and eventually reached the military hospital in Caserta on 26 July. He had become gravely ill by this time, his wound was infected and he had developed a fever. Alan Hill writes that, on his arrival at the hospital, he was met by a Leeds medical orderly, Corporal Henty, who asked him his name. 'When he gave it I remarked, "Are you the Yorkshire cricketer?" He replied, "Yes, that's me." Immediately there was a great bond of sympathy between us because Hedley Verity was a name to conjure with,' Henty recalled.

Verity was operated on three days later to remove part of a broken rib that was pressing against his lung. The operation was carried out with great skill, though only a local anaesthetic was used. At first the operation appeared to have been successful, but he then suffered the first of three haemorrhages. Verity remained conscious throughout and, according to Corporal Henty, was looking forward to his repatriation. 'We took him out onto the veranda into the warm sunshine as often as we could,' he said. It was clear, however, that he was growing weaker by the hour, and barely two days after the operation, on the afternoon of Saturday, 31 July, Verity passed away. He was 38.

There was a sombre postscript to Verity's death, involving the South African cricket writer Louis Duffus. He was working as a war correspondent, based in Egypt during that time, and had driven to a military hospital on the North African coast to interview the Eastern Province cricketer, Des Dimbleby. He had been in action with a British unit on 20 July when Verity was wounded, and informed Duffus that he had since learned of the Englishmen's death. 'I mentioned it in my writing,' Duffus related, 'and was later told by a Cairo censor that it was the first news received of the death of the England bowler, a gentle and endearing person with whom I had travelled round South Africa during the 1938–39 tour.'

The news, when it was confirmed in England on 3 September 1943, was received with great shock and sadness. Yardley described it as a 'crippling loss' and, in a glowing tribute, wrote, 'England lost perhaps the greatest cricketer of the inter-war period, modest, thoughtful, greatest in the greatest crisis, a man who never did a bad turn to anyone on the field, and who was liked and trusted by everyone who knew him.' In an age when England were captained only by amateurs, the arch-autocrat Douglas Jardine even advanced the claims of Verity, describing him once as 'the oldest head on young shoulders in English cricket'. He would have been almost 41 by the start of the 1946 season, but so finely tuned was his bowling that the batsman Arthur Mitchell had no doubt he would have continued to exert his powerful influence: 'I had made up my mind that Hedley was booked to play for Yorkshire until he was 50.'

In 40 Tests the 'scholarly' Verity took 144 wickets at 24.37 apiece. He was at his most irresistible at Lord's in 1934 when, in a single afternoon on a rain-affected surface, he routed Australia to capture 14 wickets for 80 runs. Yet for all his success, Cardus noted that, 'He preferred to go to work on a flawless Australian wicket against Bradman than revel in a "sticky" pitch where the batsmen could set him few problems.' His 766 balls in the timeless Test (95.6 eight-ball overs) pushed that inclination to its limits, and stood as a record for 17 years until overtaken by the West Indian Sonny Ramadhin (774) against England at Birmingham in May 1957. Twice Verity took ten wickets in an innings: against Warwickshire at Headingly in 1931, for 36 runs in 18.4 overs, and against Nottinghamshire, at the same venue a year later, for ten runs in 19.4 overs. The latter is a world record in first-class cricket for the fewest number of runs conceded by a bowler taking ten wickets in an innings, and included the hat-trick. In all first-class cricket he amassed 1,956 wickets, of which 1,558 were taken for Yorkshire at 13.71.

If there was a criticism of Verity it was said that he sometimes pushed the ball through too quickly, at the expense of flight and guile, and could appear almost mechanical in the process. Robertson-Glasgow, an unqualified admirer, would hear none of it and, in one perfectly pitched paragraph, succeeded in encompassing all the virtues of Verity, the bowler and the man:

> Some say Verity is not a great bowler. They are wrong. I have had heard such adjectives as 'good' and 'mechanical' applied to him. The first is merely inadequate, the second is true in so far that he is nearly the perfect bowling machine directed

by one of the most acute brains the game has known and kept in motion, against the best batsmen, by an indomitable courage.

ENGLAND

Walter Reginald Hammond (1903–65)

Gloucestershire

Record in the timeless Test: scored 164 runs, including 140 in the second innings. Bowled 23 overs without a wicket, and held one catch.

Hammond was commissioned as a Pilot Officer in the RAF after joining up in October 1939 at the age of 36. His duties were purely of an administrative capacity and it allowed him to play as much cricket as was possible. On one occasion, in Egypt, he found himself up against his old foe, Dudley Nourse. On another, stationed in South Africa, he renewed rivalries with Norman Gordon, a bowler for whom his high opinion never wavered. Cricket thrived during the war years and participation was not frowned upon as it had been in 1914, when it was deemed deeply unpatriotic to play while men were dying in the trenches. The game in England was identified as a morale booster, an entertainment and relaxation, and an effective means of raising money for war charities to boot. 'It was realised by the Government, and by the Services, that cricket provided a healthy and restful antidote to war strain,' Pelham Warner wrote.

Hammond excelled at one-day cricket and, in the words of the author David Foot, 'He simply batted from memory. He seldom tried too hard – and he seldom failed. The spectators were never let down.' For the most part, Hammond had what might be described as a comfortable war. His was not, as Howat put it, 'a war in which he had to face the enemy with the courage of, say, Edrich or the sacrifice of Verity or Farnes'. Nonetheless, he played his part and had attained the rank of Squadron Leader before he was discharged in 1944 on medical grounds.

He headed the batting averages for the eighth successive season when full-time cricket returned in 1946, hitting 1,783 runs at 84.90 and captaining England to victory over India in three Tests. His game showed no obvious diminution in skill and he was the automatic choice to lead his country that winter in the first Ashes series for eight years, despite at 43 being the oldest man to captain an England side to Australia. Many were resistant to England touring so soon after the war, but he had no doubts and saw the venture as 'a goodwill mission'. A combination of events, however, conspired to turn it into a sad decline and failure for Hammond: a tour too far.

England suffered a humiliating reverse in the opening Test in Brisbane, when they appeared wholly unprepared for the no-holds-barred brand of cricket played by Bradman's Australia, and lost the second in Sydney. In England's defence the umpiring was abysmal and the tourists, inevitably perhaps, did not receive the rub of the green. Moreover, there were grumblings in the press about Hammond's age. His complex private life was catching up with him, and his wife had started divorce proceedings. During the tour of South Africa in 1938–39 he had met and fallen for a Durban beauty queen, Sybil Ness-Harvey, who would become his second wife. She had come to England and was homesick and lonely on her own without him; her welfare weighed heavily on his mind. The captaincy that he had once worn so lightly in South Africa rapidly became a burden: he was tactically outsmarted by Bradman, and the runs dried up. Even Bill Edrich, the staunchest of friends, found him 'edgy, retiring and irritable'.

The third and fourth Tests were drawn and, with Australia having already retained the Ashes, Hammond left himself out of the side for the fifth. The fibrositis that had precipitated his discharge from the RAF was causing him acute pain and could only be quelled by aspirin. Yardley assumed the captaincy but was unable to prevent Australia from taking the series 3–0.

Hammond returned to make 79 against New Zealand in a rain-effected Test in Christchurch (he was cheered all the way to the wicket), and arrived back in England to announce his retirement with immediate effect.

Aside from an ill-conceived comeback at 48 for Gloucestershire against Somerset in 1951 when – to the great sadness of players and spectators alike – he could barely lay bat on ball, that was it from a batsman who, in the words of Robertson-Glasgow, 'enriched the game with a grace, a simplicity and a nobility that may never be seen again'. In 85 Tests he scored 7,249 runs at 58.45, with 22 centuries, and took 83 wickets; in all first-class matches there were 50,551 runs, 732 wickets and 820 catches. He became the first batsman to score 6,000 runs in Test cricket, a feat he achieved during the tour of South Africa in 1938–39 on the opening day of the rubber in Johannesburg. In 20 Tests as England captain, he won four, lost three and drew 13. He died of a heart attack in South Africa on 19 July 1965, aged 62, after moving to Durban with his second wife in 1951.

Len Hutton (1916–90)

Yorkshire

Record in the timeless Test: scored 93 runs, including 55 in the second innings. Bowled one over without a wicket, and took one catch.

Hutton's 364 against Australia at The Oval in 1938 would have been enough to assure him cricketing immortality alone, but not content with that he went on to become England's first regular professional captain and the man who won back the Ashes after a wait of almost 20 years. There were further significant achievements: he was the first professional elected to life membership of MCC while still playing, and the second to be knighted for his services to cricket, after Jack Hobbs. As if that was not enough, he overcame a potentially career-threatening injury sustained in 1941 while serving as a Sergeant in the Army Physical Training Corps.

He fractured his left arm when a mat slipped from under him in the gymnasium and was forced to spend eight months in hospital. He underwent three complicated bone grafts to repair the damage, and was eventually discharged from hospital with his left arm two inches shorter than the other. 'When I saw my arm after all those plaster encasements and complete inactivity,' he wrote, 'it was reduced to the size of a boy's.' Despite months of rehabilitation, massage and remedial exercise, his return to full-time cricket with his technique unimpaired (though he had to dispense with the hook shot altogether) was testament to his supreme ability and unfailing determination. 'In the hall of fame,' *Wisden* wrote, 'he sits at the high table with the elite.'

Hutton enjoyed a truly golden summer in 1949, scoring 3,429 runs at 68.58, with 12 centuries, and passing a thousand runs in both June and August; for England he formed a formidable opening partnership with the Lancastrian, Cyril Washbrook. His elevation to the captaincy arrived three years later, against India at Leeds, though he presumed that he was merely keeping the seat warm until someone else came along. Instead, he captained his country in another 22 Tests, winning 13, drawing six and losing only four – an outstanding record. England won back the Ashes under him at The Oval in 1953 amidst unforgettable scenes, and retained them in Australia two years later, with Frank Tyson as a lightning-quick spearhead.

Hutton was dropped only once by England – against Australia in 1948 (after receiving a thorough working over from Keith Miller and Ray Lindwall) – and did not miss another Test until his enforced retirement with chronic back pain in 1955; the problem had first surfaced on tour in South Africa in 1938–39. He was knighted in the summer of 1956. In 79 Tests he scored 6,971 runs at 56.67, including 19 centuries, and 40,140 in all first-class cricket, reaching his hundredth hundred in 619 innings. His son Richard, an all-rounder, played five Tests for England in 1971, an achievement that was said to have given Hutton senior more pleasure than anything else. He served as a Test selector in 1975–76, but suffered from poor health in later years and died in Kingston-upon-Thames, aged 74.

William John Edrich (1916–86)

Middlesex and Norfolk

Record in the timeless Test: scored 220 runs, including 219 in the second innings. Bowled 15 overs without a wicket, and held one catch.

Edrich's was a remarkable war. He went from Pilot Officer to acting Squadron Leader in a matter of days, earned legendary status among air-crews and superiors alike in Bomber Command for his death-defying skill and bravery, and was awarded the Distinguished Flying Cross. He flew in the daylight raid by Bristol Blenheims on the Cologne power stations, Knapsack and Quadrath, on 12 August 1941 – a mission that was described by one newspaper as 'the RAF's most audacious and dangerous low-level bombing raid'. The casualty rate among bomber pilots was severe and, in the attack on Cologne, 12 of the 54 Blenheims failed to return. Edrich, to his unceasing relief, cheated death more times than he cared to remember, and as a consequence always lived his life to the full. His appetite for a good night out never palled and often landed him in trouble with the cricketing authorities.

The 'profound remorse at losing so many fine friends' also stayed with him for ever.

A fierce patriot, Edrich played his cricket with the same fearlessness and indifference to danger and, on his return to Test cricket in the ill-fated Australia tour of 1946–47, bore the brunt of Keith Miller and Ray Lindwall at their fastest, scoring 462 runs. Interestingly, after the selectors failed to pick him for the series against West Indies in 1939, he was also excluded from the England team that played India in 1946 and was by no means a unanimous selection for Australia. He became an amateur after the war, and it was during the 1946–47 tour, *Wisden* asserted, that 'he showed himself indisputably as a Test player'. His crowning achievement as a cricketer came in 1947 when he hit 3,539 runs at an average of 80.43 and took 67 wickets; there were also 552 runs in four Tests against South Africa that summer, before more carousing cost him his England place again. In this particular incident, during a series against West Indies in 1950, he had to be helped to his room by the night porter and succeeded in waking up the chairman of selectors next door. His various run-ins with authority made him, in the words of Ralph Barker, 'a controversial cricketer'.

Yet Edrich was back at the crease, unbeaten on 55, when the Ashes were reclaimed in 1953 and played his 39th and final Test against Australia at Adelaide in

1955. He scored 2,440 runs at 40 – his 219 in the timeless Test remained his highest Test score – and picked up 41 wickets. In all first-class cricket he hit 36,965 runs and took 479 wickets. After signing off at Middlesex he captained Norfolk, the county of his birth, from 1959 to 1972, eventually retiring at 56. He died after a fall at his home in Chesham, Buckinghamshire, aged 70, having attended a St George's Day lunch; a patriot to the end. As he put it once: 'I feel that I have been so lucky. A farmer's boy came to Lord's and reaped such a rich harvest.'

Leslie Ethelbert George Ames (1905–90)

Kent

Record in the timeless Test: scored 101 runs, including
84 in the first innings. Held two catches and
conceded only six byes.

The imperturbable Ames was England's first-choice wicketkeeper from 1931 to 1939 until a back injury determined that he played solely as a batsman, a role for which he was more than adept. He made his final appearance for England in the timeless Test, though there was an offer of more international cricket after the war. Hammond wanted him in his side to tour Australia in 1946–47 as a batsman but, despite holding the England captain in the highest esteem, he could not be persuaded to travel. He was an essential part of Kent's championship side from 1927 to 1951, before a recurrence of back trouble brought his career to an abrupt close. By that time he had stockpiled 37,248 runs, made 102 hundreds, nine double-hundreds, exceeded a thousand runs a season on 17 occasions and pulled off 418 stumpings, almost apologetically, so it was said. His wicketkeeping was described by *Wisden* as neat and economical, with 'no flamboyant gestures'. In South Africa in 1938–39, he conceded only one bye for every 275 balls bowled during the series, while there were few batsmen in the world capable of hitting the ball harder or in such classical style.

In 47 Tests he scored 2,434 runs at 40.56 and struck eight centuries; he caught 74 batsmen and stumped 23. He was the first professional to be appointed a Test selector – a task he performed for eight seasons from 1950 – and was manager on three MCC tours. During the war he joined the RAF and, in an administrative capacity, rose to the rank of Squadron Leader. He died in Canterbury on 27 February 1990, aged 84.

Edward Paynter (1901–79)

Lancashire

Record in the timeless Test: scored 137 runs, hitting 62 and 75, and held two catches.

The war robbed Paynter of the last few precious years of his first-class career. He was 37 and still an England player at its outset, and almost 44 when it ended. He was a relatively late starter anyway, and didn't score his first century for Lancashire until 1931, by which time he was 30; his Test debut followed that summer against New Zealand. He proceeded, nevertheless, to make a substantial impact. In 20 Tests he hit 1,540 runs at an average of 59.23, including double-hundreds against both Australia – he averaged a remarkable 84.42 in seven Tests against them – and South Africa. He was a brilliant fieldsman, too, despite losing the top joints to the index and middle fingers of his right hand in an accident as a youth.

He won everlasting fame when, in the fourth Test against Australia at Brisbane in 1933, he rose from his hospital bed (he was suffering from tonsillitis) to rescue England with a battling 83. He valiantly refused a runner and, during a brief second-innings knock, finished the match with a six. He was also the victim of a cowardly assault during the series when a group of men deliberately knocked him down from behind while walking to the Adelaide Oval, leaving him sprawled on the pavement.

After the war he resisted several requests from Lancashire to return but, in 1947 during two festival matches at Harrogate, compiled scores of 154, 73 and

127 (the latter in only 85 minutes) to suggest that his run-making abilities were far from undimmed. In all first-class cricket he scored 20,075 runs at 42.26 with 45 centuries, and played his last Test match against West Indies at Old Trafford in July 1939. His 653 runs at 81.62 on the 1938–39 tour remained a record for an Englishman in South Africa until eclipsed by Andrew Strauss (656) in 2005. Paynter, who did not serve during the war, died in Keighley, Yorkshire, on 5 February 1979, aged 77. To *Wisden*, he was simply 'a wonderful cricketer'.

Paul Anthony Gibb (1913–77)

Cambridge University, Scotland, Yorkshire and Essex

Record in the timeless Test: scored 124 runs, including 120 in second innings. Relieved Ames of the gloves in final session during sixth day.

After enlisting in the RAF during the war, when he piloted Coastal Command Sunderland flying-boats, Gibb returned to the Yorkshire side in 1946 after an absence from the game of seven years. He was 32 at the time but appeared still to have plenty of cricket left in him. So much so that he was selected to keep wicket in the first two Tests of the summer against India, and made 60 at Lord's batting at No. 6. He was included in Hammond's side to tour Australia in

1946–47 but, after being preferred to the technically superior Godfrey Evans for the first Test, endured a horrible match behind the stumps. He was promptly dropped and never played for England again. He was not the most naturally gifted of wicketkeepers it has to be said, and it was the journalist William Pollock who suggested during the 1938–39 tour of South Africa that, 'he is better at fielding well away from the wickets than he is behind them'.

After the tour of Australia, Gibb disappeared from the game for four years before reappearing for Essex as a professional, becoming the first cricket blue to abdicate his amateur status. During that time his form, both behind the stumps and with the bat, was good enough to earn him a Test trial at the age of 40 in 1953. He retired three years later and from 1957 to 1966 was a first-class umpire, living a somewhat nomadic and unconventional existence while he carried out his duties, driving from ground to ground in an old van with a caravan in tow.

The bespectacled Gibb bore more than a passing resemblance to Geoff Boycott during his younger days, though in deference to Boycott the similarity ends there. In eight Tests Gibb scored 581 runs at 44.69 with two centuries, both against South Africa, and 12,520 in first-class cricket; he caught 425 batsmen and stumped 123. He was working as a bus driver in Guildford when he died suddenly on 7 December 1977, aged 64. He never talked about his past and many of his colleagues were surprised to learn that he had played cricket for England. He was erroneously excluded from *Wisden's* obituary section the following year.

Bryan Herbert Valentine (1908–83)

Cambridge University and Kent

Record in the timeless Test: scored 30 runs in two innings, and was at the crease with Ames when the game was abandoned.

Valentine played no more Test cricket after the 1938–39 tour of South Africa. He was 37 when he resumed playing for Kent in 1946 and no longer under consideration as an England player. Like so many batsmen of that era, his Test opportunities were limited by the superfluity of talent available to the selectors. One of a long line of gifted and popular amateur strokemakers, in which Kent specialised, he captained his county for three years before retiring at the end of the 1948 season. He ended his first-class career on 18,306 runs at 30.15 with 35 hundreds. His Test record was far more impressive: 454 runs at almost 65 with two centuries. He made his highest Test score against India in 1933, hitting 136 on his debut in Bombay, and was selected for all five Tests in South Africa, completing 275 runs at 68.75, including a brazen 112 in the second Test at Newlands. A Lieutenant in the Queen's Own Royal West Kent Regiment, he served in North Africa with distinction and won the Military Cross. He died in Otford, Kent, aged 75.

Douglas Vivian Parson Wright (1914–98)

Kent

Record in the timeless Test: bowled 69 overs for five wickets, including second-innings figures of three for 146. Scored 26 runs in England's first innings.

Wright was in his early thirties when the war finished and continued to propel his leg-breaks on and off for another five years in Test cricket. He made his last appearance for England in 1951 against New Zealand at Wellington's Basin Reserve, capturing five for 48 in a six-wicket victory. He finished with 108 Test wickets at 39.11, and 2,056 in all. He claimed his best Test figures of seven for 105 against Australia in the fifth Test at Sydney on the 1946–47 tour, bowling Bradman for 12 in the first innings and having him dropped at slip by Edrich on two in the second, when for just a brief and tantalising moment – it was no more – it looked as though he might win the game for

England. He was a highly dangerous bowler on his day but, as *Wisden* is at pains to point out, there could also be days of 'abject frustration' and ultimately he promised more than he delivered. When he did it get it right, he was unplayable, as his record of seven first-class hat-tricks handsomely testifies. It was to his credit, also, that it was said of him he never bowled a ball defensively; 'every ball was bowled to take a wicket'. Bradman retained a healthy regard for his bowling, and his was one of the first names opposing batsmen always looked for whenever an England side was announced. He was appointed Kent's first professional captain in 1954 and retired three years later to take up coaching. He died in Canterbury, aged 84.

Reginald Thomas David Perks (1911–77)

Worcestershire

Record in the timeless Test: bowled 73 overs for six wickets, including first-innings figures of five for 100 on his debut. Scored two runs.

As a cricketer Perks had more reason than most to lament his six lost years. He was 28 at the outbreak of war and 'almost true fast in pace', in the words of John Arlott, having just embarked on his Test career. When the sport recommenced he was nearly 35 and, for a bowler of his type, past his prime. During the 1939 season he took 159 first-class wickets, adding materially to his reputation, and in only a couple of Tests, against South Africa and West Indies, claimed two impressive five-wicket hauls. In the last of those two matches, 'on a deadly easy wicket' at The Oval, Arlott noted that 'he never bowled better and generated quite remarkable pace'. Tall and powerfully built, Perks played for another nine years after the war, taking a hundred wickets a season on 16 occasions, including nine consecutively from 1946 to 1955. In 595 first-class games he claimed 2,233 wickets at 24.07, and 11 in two Tests at 32.27. He died unexpectedly, aged 66, in Worcester.

The Men Who Sat Out the Timeless Test

Norman Yardley, England's perennial 12th man in South Africa, succeeded Hammond as captain of his country, leading the side against South Africa in 1947 and Australia the following year. He captained England in 14 of his 20 Tests, scoring 812 runs with a highest score of 99 against the Springboks at Nottingham; in all, he hit 18,173 runs at 31.17 and took 279 wickets. He was a brave batsman and a handy medium-pacer who once dismissed Bradman in three successive innings. He joined the Green Howards in the war, serving in the Middle East and Italy. He died of a stroke, aged 74, in 1989. His great friend Hugh Bartlett was selected to tour India with MCC in 1939–40 and would almost certainly have won a Test cap in that series but for the war. He captained Sussex from 1947 to 1949 and scored 10,098 first-class runs in 216 matches. He collapsed and died while watching a Sunday League match at Hove in 1988, aged 73. Bartlett served in the Glider Pilot Regiment, and was awarded the Distinguished Flying Cross at Arnhem.

The off-spinner Tom Goddard appeared twice for England against West Indies in 1939, finishing with 22 wickets at 26.72 from eight Tests. He continued to play for Gloucestershire after the war and retired in 1952 at the age of 51. He took 2,979 wickets at 19.84, claiming one hundred or more in a season on 16 occasions, during a period when off-break bowling was often seen as an unfashionable adjunct to leg-spin. He died in 1966, aged 65. The leg-spinner Len Wilkinson never fulfilled the rich promise he showed in 1938 when, at the age of 21, he captured 151 wickets in his 'once-in-a-lifetime' first season for Lancashire. Only Yorkshire's Wilfred Rhodes, with 154 wickets in 1898 when he was 20, took more at a younger age. There were 63 wickets in 1939 for Wilkinson but, according to *Wisden*, he was virtually unrecognisable as the same bowler. He suffered a serious knee injury in the opening game of the 1946 season at Fenner's and managed only two more appearances for his county, retiring to the leagues and a newsagent's. He played three Tests, all against South Africa, taking seven wickets at 38.71, and died in 2002, aged 85[1].

SOUTH AFRICA

Alan Melville (1910–83)

Natal, Oxford University, Sussex and Transvaal

Record in the timeless Test: scored 181 runs,
hitting 78 and 103.

Melville's Test career resumed in 1947 when he led a raw and experimental party to England on what was South Africa's first post-war tour. His presence in the side, however, had been a cause for some concern. He had spent a year in a steel jacket, recovering from a fall while training with the South African forces in the war. Injury-plagued at the best of times, there had been fears he might never play again. They were swiftly dispelled. Melville revelled in the role of elder statesman on tour – he was 37 by then – and scored centuries in the first two Tests: 189 and an unbeaten 104 at Nottingham, and 117 at Lord's. As he had also scored 103 during the timeless Test in his last innings for South Africa before the war, he became the first man to record four consecutive hundreds against England, albeit ones that extended over two series and were eight years apart. He hit 569 runs in the five Tests at 63.22 and 1,547 in all games, including six centuries.

It was his pinnacle as a Test batsman, though he had not been without his health problems on tour, and South Africa lost three Tests. Melville was never robust physically and the toll of captaincy exhausted him to the extent that he was reported to have lost nearly two stone by the time he returned home. It came as no surprise when he announced his retirement shortly afterwards. Yet two years later he was persuaded to play in the third Test against George Mann's England side at Newlands. It was a brief comeback: he scored 15 and 24, and the former South African batsman Jackie McGlew admitted that, 'Melville's unexpected return to the fold, in his only Test in which he was not captain, was disappointing by his own high standards.' Nonetheless, he added, 'The seasons in which he played fell in a magic era – rich and glamorous and, in their own way, a golden portion of South African cricket history.'

The side Melville led to England in 1947 lost nothing in the popularity stakes with their 1935 predecessors, and rarely failed to create a favourable impression on or off the field. In addition, they brought over a supply of canned food 'as a gesture of sympathy' when rationing was at its most swingeing, and contributed half their share of the gate against Surrey and Lancashire to help with the rebuilding of their bomb-damaged grounds. Melville scored 894 runs at 52.58 in 11 Tests – all against England – and 10,958 in 190 first-class matches. He died in 1983, aged 72.

Arthur Dudley Nourse (1910–81)

Natal

Record in the timeless Test: scored 128 runs, including 103 in first innings.

Nourse succeeded Melville as captain of South Africa in 1948. His record was not a glorious one: in two series against England and one against Australia, he lost nine and won one. Yet his batting never failed him; his special glory, *Wisden* wrote, was the square-cut. There were 536 runs in ten innings against the 1948–49 England tourists in his first series as captain, and a further 405 against Lindsay Hassett's Australians during which he topped the South African batting averages for the fifth successive season. He was 40 when he bowed out as captain against England in 1951 and achieved his solitary victory under the most unlikely of circumstances.

He had suffered a broken thumb while fielding in the game at Bristol three weeks before the first Test, an injury that threatened to put him out of the series. He was told by a surgeon that if his thumb was plastered he would miss at least two months of the tour. The only other option was to pin the bone, which would at least enable him to play in the first Test at Nottingham, but would prove agonisingly painful. Naturally, Nourse chose the second option and proceeded to play a match-winning innings of 'unprecedented courage'. He scored 208, occupying the crease for more than nine hours, mostly in severe pain, especially when he tried to impart any power into his shots – a pronounced drawback for such a muscular striker of the ball. According to *Wisden*, he refused to have an injection to relieve the pain because he feared it would numb his hand and affect his grip. He was unable to bat in South Africa's second innings, but the tourists bowled out England for 114 and won an amazing Test by 71 runs.

Nourse's Test record is up there with the very best: 2,960 runs at 53.81, with nine centuries, from 34 matches; there were 12,472 runs in all and 41 hundreds. Only Graeme Pollock and Jacques Kallis among South African Test batsmen have a superior average. He enlisted in the army during the war and served in the Western Desert. He died in Durban at the age of 70.

Bruce Mitchell (1909–95)

Transvaal

Record in the timeless Test: scored 100 runs, including 89 in second innings. Bowled 44 overs for one wicket.

Mitchell was a tireless cornerstone of South African batting for nearly all of his 42 Tests, at a time when his country's resources were often alarmingly thin. The role carried such great responsibility that it contributed in no small part to his reputation – a somewhat unfair one – of being a dour, strokeless batsman. In fact, he possessed all the strokes; he just didn't always get the chance to put them on display. On one occasion in England he was barracked by an irate spectator, who accused him of doing a passable impression of a monument. He was often immovable. His third trip to England in 1947 was a particularly fruitful one and he scored 597 runs at 61.03 in five Tests. At The Oval he batted for more than 13 hours to score 120 and 189, becoming the second South African after Melville to hit a century in each innings of a Test. He collected his seventh century against England in the 1948–49 series, and missed out on an eighth when he was dismissed for 99 in the fifth Test.

No one would have predicted, however, that he had just played his final game for South Africa. It was the arrival of Miller and Lindwall a year later that triggered his sensational omission from the side, after being ruthlessly targeted by the pair while playing for Transvaal. It brought this sequence of 42 consecutive Tests to an abrupt end and, in *Wisden's* view, amounted to 'the shabbiest treatment handed out to a Springbok by selectors'. Mitchell played no more first-class cricket after that, finishing with 3,471 Test runs at an average of 48.88, with 27 wickets, a record that puts him among the forefront of South African cricketers. He served with the Transvaal Scottish Regiment in the war and fought at El Alamein. He died in Johannesburg, aged 86. The last word belongs to *Wisden*: 'Few quieter or more modest men have played Test cricket, and Mitchell's perfect sportsmanship on and off the field at all times was living proof that success can be achieved without any compromise of behaviour.'

Eric Alfred Burchell Rowan (1909–93)

Eastern Province and Transvaal

Record in the timeless Test: scored 33 runs, and took one catch.

Rowan was the complete antithesis of Mitchell: tempestuous, brash and with a complete disregard for authority. He was, naturally enough, a highly combative cricketer who, when he was not falling in and out of scrapes with the selectors – or his fellow players – continued to flourish in Test cricket until he was 42. It was said that personality clashes kept him out of the tour to England in 1947, but he was recalled in 1948–49 and, after failing in the first Test, struck an undefeated 156 at Johannesburg in the second. Unfortunately the selectors, acting in haste, had already named the side for the third Test against England before Rowan completed his second-innings century, replacing him with Melville, who was making his comeback. As Rowan returned to the pavilion at the conclusion of his innings, he is reputed to have made a V-sign in the general direction of the selectors. He explained later that it was actually a V for Victory sign (the match was drawn); when informed that it was the wrong way round, he replied, 'That depends on what part of the ground you're sitting.' The matter was resolved and Rowan returned to the side for the fourth and fifth Tests.

He was vice-captain to Nourse in England in 1951 when he scored 236 in the fourth Test at Leeds to become the oldest South African to record a double-century in Test cricket (he was 42). He played his final Test in that series at The Oval, scoring 55 and 45. He enlisted in the army in 1939 and rose to the rank of Lieutenant. He was the elder brother of the off-spinner Athol Rowan, who represented South Africa in 15 Tests. Eric Rowan scored

1,965 runs at 43.66 in 26 Tests, and probably should have toured Australia in 1952–53. His appetite for runs remained undiminished, though perhaps the selectors felt that enough was enough. He died in Johannesburg, aged 83, a fully paid-up member of the awkward squad.

Kenneth George Viljoen (1910–74)

Griqualand West, Orange Free State and Transvaal

Record in the timeless Test: scored 74 in the second innings after being dismissed for a duck in the first.

A stylish right-handed batsman, Viljoen played in 27 Tests but it was as an administrator that he made his most significant contribution to South African cricket. He will also be remembered as the man who needed two haircuts during the timeless Test. He managed the Springboks on two successful tours to Australia, in 1952–53 and 1963–64, and one to England in 1955, achieving a reputation as a firm but fair disciplinarian. The Springboks drew both series in Australia, much against expectation, and lost only narrowly, 3–2, to England. John Arlott wrote later that the principles he established on those tours – a great emphasis was put on fielding – did much to establish South Africa's pre-eminence in world cricket during the 1960s. Viljoen toured England for the second time in 1947 when his experience was a boon to Melville, and played his last

Test, also against England, at Port Elizabeth two years later. He was a brilliant outfielder whose 27 Tests realised 1,365 runs at 28.43, and included two centuries. He died in Krugersdorp, Transvaal, aged 63.

Eric Londesbrough Dalton (1906–81)

Natal

Record in the timeless Test: scored 78 runs, including 57 in first innings. Bowled 40 overs for six wickets, including first-innings figures of four for 59, and held one catch.

Dalton was 40 when cricket resumed again and his Test days, sadly, were behind him. He will be remembered as a crunching middle-order strokemaker and a useful leg-spinner, who had a habit of picking up important wickets (Hammond succumbed to him twice in the timeless Test, stumped on both occasions) and for disposing of irksome partnerships. He averaged 44 in the 1938–39 series, including a century in the first Test in Johannesburg, where he wielded his heavy bat to resounding effect in the extreme altitude. The England players – and Farnes in particular – rated him highly, as much for his attitude as anything: Test cricket was just another game to him. An amiable character, Dalton toured England twice, in 1929 and 1935, and played in 15 Tests, scoring 698 runs at 31.72 and capturing

12 wickets at 40.83 apiece. He died in Durban at the age of 74. He is celebrated as one of South Africa's finest all-round sportsmen: an amateur golf champion (1950) and an accomplished tennis, table-tennis player and footballer. In addition he was a fine baritone and played the piano – brilliantly, of course.

Pieter Gerhard Vintcent van der Bijl (1907–73)

Oxford University and Western Province

Record in the timeless Test: scored 222 runs, hitting 125 and 97.

Despite only a modest career as a varsity cricketer – some thought him a better boxer – the towering Van der Bijl went on to play in five Tests against England and score 460 runs at a highly respectable 51. Ponderous in style he may have been, but as an opening batsman he lacked for nothing in courage or determination. 'It has always puzzled me what the meaning of eternity is,' he is reported to have said after the timeless Test. 'Now I have a good idea.' He missed out by three runs in that match on becoming the first South African to score a century in each innings of a Test, falling to the softest of dismissals off the bowling of Wright. He was a Captain in the Duke of Edinburgh's Own Rifles, later promoted to Lieutenant Colonel, and awarded the Military Cross. On one occasion in North Africa, he commanded an armoured car across several hundred yards of exposed desert terrain to retrieve half-a-dozen wounded infantrymen from under the nose of the German artillery.

He was badly wounded in Italy and invalided out of the army in 1943; his injuries prevented him from playing any further first-class cricket after the war. He returned to his post as a schoolmaster and also acted as a selector and cricket administrator. His son Vintcent was a formidable fast-medium bowler whose career coincided with the years South Africa spent in sporting isolation, and is regarded as one of the best cricketers never to have played in a Test. Pieter van der Bijl scored 2,692 runs in all first-class cricket, and died of a heart attack in Cape Town at the age of 65.

Ronald Eustace Grieveson (1909–98)

Transvaal

Record in the timeless Test: scored 114 runs, including 75 in first innings. Completed three stumpings, and held two catches.

In the space of just two Tests, Grieveson established himself as one of South Africa's most influential and indispensable cricketers. He conceded only 15 byes in England's aggregate of 970 runs in the timeless Test, while his 75 runs in the Springboks' first innings (he did not bat in his first Test in Johannesburg) was the highest debut score by a wicketkeeper in a Test at that point. His genuine enthusiasm at playing for his country was reflected in his cricket, and his natural exuberance behind the stumps or with the bat rapidly rubbed off on the rest of the XI. The timeless Test left him far from surfeited. 'What a game,' was how he liked to remember it. Louis Duffus called his wicketkeeping 'high-class' and instantly identified him as a 'key player'; Farnes considered him as good a bat as any in the South African side. However, as he was nearly 30 when he debuted in Johannesburg, the war effectively put an end to his international career. He scored 114 runs in two Test innings at an average of 57, and completed seven catches and three stumpings. During the war, Grieveson joined the army and rose to the rank of major, winning an OBE for his services. He was later a selector for several years, and died in Johannesburg, aged 88.

Edward Serrurier Newson (1910–88)

Transvaal and Rhodesia

Record in the timeless Test: bowled 68.6 overs for two wickets, and scored four runs.

In terms of runs per over, 'Bob' Newson was South Africa's most economical bowler in the timeless Test, delivering 68.6 overs at a cost of 149 runs. A somewhat peripatetic right-arm fast bowler, his three Test appearances were spread over nine years after making his debut against England in 1930 at the Wanderers. Bizarrely, the selectors neglected to inform him of his selection and he had turned up to work as usual on the morning of the Test. There was a frantic rush to get him to the ground on time. South Africa won narrowly by 28 runs and, after failing to capture a wicket, Newson was dropped. He dropped out of the game for almost eight years after that, reappearing for South Africa in the fourth Test against England in 1939. After the war he moved to Rhodesia and in 1949 recorded his best bowling figures of five for 54 against MCC in Bulawayo. He claimed four Test wickets at 56 apiece, and 60 in 24 first-class matches. He died in Durban, aged 77.

Norman Gordon (1911–2014)

Transvaal

Record in the timeless Test: bowled 92.2 overs for
one wicket. Scored seven runs, and held the catch
that dismissed Edrich for 219.

When the 17-man Springbok party to tour England in 1947 was announced, Gordon's name was missing. The side was decidedly light on pace bowlers, and the three chosen – Lindsay Tuckett, Ossie Dawson and Jack Plimsoll – could not muster a Test cap between them; instead the selectors had packed the team with spinners. A convincing case could have been made for Gordon's inclusion, particularly as there was no 'Chud' Langton to call on any more. He was still fit, capable of bowling for long spells and made no secret of his eagerness to tour. More significantly, he was a proven Test cricketer and conditions in England would have been much to his liking.

Gordon always believed, however, that his omission had less to do with cricket and more to do with the fact he was Jewish; and that Melville didn't want to risk taking him on tour. The matter still appeared raw 64 years later. 'A friend of mine told me he had heard from one of the selectors that Melville had advised them not to select me as there might be anti-Semitism and unpleasantness in England,' he explained in an interview with the *Daily Telegraph* in 2011. 'He thought it expedient to leave me out. There was quite a bit of feeling about Jews in England even after the war.' British soldiers were being killed on the streets of Palestine, and their deaths were a part of the general despair, exhaustion, hunger and frayed tempers that beset bombed-out Britain in 1947.

Gordon was proud of his faith. He wasn't the first Jew to play Test cricket for South Africa but he had been the first to openly admit to it at a time of frightening anti-Semitism. He liked to laugh off an incident during his Test debut in Johannesburg when a heckler shouted at him, 'Here comes the rabbi.' 'Fortunately I took five wickets in the innings and that shut him up for the rest of the series,' he recalled. Yet it was also true that wickets had not been in plentiful supply for him during the 1946–47 season; the selectors had picked a young side and, at nearly 36, he was no longer the future. Whatever the reasons for his exclusion in 1947 it signalled the end of his career, and he played his last game for Transvaal against George Mann's MCC tourists at Ellis Park in December 1948. Hutton wrote later that, but for the war, 'he would have made a big name for himself'.

Afterwards he ran a sports shop – Luggage Craft – on Eloff Street, one of Johannesburg's grandest thoroughfares during the forties and fifties. One of his regular customers was Ali Bacher, the future captain of South Africa, who bought his first bat there at the age of 11, hand-picked for him by Gordon. When Gordon reached his century in 2011, it was Bacher who organised the celebrations. Mike Procter, Peter and Graeme Pollock from the 1970 Springbok team of all the talents were there, as were a cohort of fast bowlers, spanning the generations: Neil Adcock, Shaun Pollock, Fanie de Villiers and Makhaya Ntini.

And it was Bacher who led the tributes in the days after Gordon's death, aged 103, on 2 September 2014, admiring him as a man 'who had a passion for cricket and always lived life to the fullest'. There were 126 wickets at 22.24 apiece in 29 first-class games, and 20 in five Tests at 40.35, though his figures were unfairly distorted by the timeless Test's indestructible pitch and cannot tell the full story of the countless close shaves and near misses: 92.2-17-256-1. 'It was like bowling on glass,' he told *SA Cricket* magazine.

Perhaps, in the end, Gordon did well to avoid the tour of 1947. It was permanent high summer for the batsmen, and the 'Middlesex Twins' Compton and Edrich especially. The South Africans renamed them the 'Terrible Twins', conceding over 2,000 runs in all to their blazing bats. The pitches were flat, the ball hardly swung and the sun never stopped shining; improbably, even the Springboks complained it was too hot. 'The crowds were existing on rations, the rocket bomb still in the ears of most folk,' Cardus wrote, and each stroke from Compton represented 'a flick of delight, a propulsion of happy, sane, healthy life'. The only things that weren't rationed that summer, it seemed, were runs. England won the series 3–0, and no one mentioned timeless Tests.

Timeless Test Scoreboard

Kingsmead, Durban, 3–14 March 1939

South Africa

*A. Melville hit wkt b Wright	78	– (6) b Fames	103
P. G. V. van der Bijl b Perks	125	– c Paynter b Wright	97
E. A. B. Rowan lbw b Perks	33	– c Edrich b Verity	0
B. Mitchell b Wright	11	– (1) hit wkt b Verity	89
A. D. Nourse b Perks	103	– (4) c Hutton b Fames	25
K. G. Viljoen c Ames b Perks	0	– (5) b Perks	74
E. L. Dalton c Ames b Fames	57	– c and b Wright	21
†R. E. Grieveson b Perks	75	– b Fames	39
A. C. B. Langton c Paynter b Verity	27	– c Hammond b Fames	6
E. S. Newson c and b Verity	1	– b Wright	3
N. Gordon not out	0	– not out	7
B 2, lb 12, nb 6	20	B 5, lb 8, nb 4	17

1/131 (1) 2/219 (3)   (202.6 overs) 530
3/236 (4) 4/274 (2)
5/278 (6) 6/368 (7) 7/475 (5)
8/522 (8) 9/523 (10) 10/530 (9)

1/191 (1) 2/191 (3)   (142.1 overs) 481
3/191 (2) 4/242 (4)
5/346 (5) 6/382 (7) 7/434 (6)
8/450 (9) 9/462 (10) 10/481 (8)

Fames 46–9–108–1; Perks 41–5–100–5; Wright 37–6–142–2; Verity 55.6–14–97–2; Hammond 14–4–34–0; Edrich 9–2–29–0. *Second innings*—Farnes 22.1–2–74–4; Perks 32–6–99–1; Wright 32–7–146–3; Verity 40–9–87–2; Edrich 6–1–18–0; Hammond 9–1–30–0; Hutton 1–0–10–0.

England

L. Hutton run out	38	– b Mitchell	55
P. A. Gibb c Grieveson b Newson	4	– b Dalton	120
E. Paynter lbw b Langton	62	– (5) c Grieveson b Gordon	75
*W. R. Hammond st Grieveson b Dalton	24	– st Grieveson b Dalton	140
†L. E. G. Ames c Dalton b Langton	84	– (6) not out	17
W. J. Edrich c Rowan b Langton	1	– (3) c Gordon b Langton	219
B. H. Valentine st Grieveson b Dalton	26	– not out	4
H. Verity b Dalton	3		
D. V. P. Wright c Langton b Dalton	26		
K. Fames b Newson	20		
R. T. D. Perks not out	2		
B 7, lb 17, w 1, nb 1	26	B 8, lb 12, w 1, nb 3	24

1/9 (2) 2/64 (1) 3/125 (4)   (117.6 overs) 316
4/169 (3) 5/171 (6) 6/229 (7)
7/245 (8) 8/276 (5) 9/305 (9) 10/316 (10)

1/78 (1)   (5 wkts, 218.2 overs) 654
2/358 (2) 3/447 (3)
4/611 (5) 5/650 (4)

Newson 25.6–5–58–2; Langton 35–12–71–3: Gordon 37–7–82–0; Mitchell 7–0–20–0; Dalton 13–1–59–4. *Second innings*—Newson 43–4–91–0; Gordon 55.2–10–174–1; Langton 56–12–132–1; Dalton 27–3–100–2; Mitchell 37–4–133–1.

Umpires: R. G. A. Ashman and G. L. Sickler.

Close of play: first day, South Africa 229-2 (Van der Bijl 105, Mitchell 4); second day, South Africa 423-6 (Nourse 77, Grieveson 26); third day, England 35-1 (Hutton 24, Paynter 6); fourth day, England 268-7 (Ames 82, Wright 5); fifth day, South Africa 193-3 (Nourse 1, Viljoen 1); sixth day, England 0-0 (Hutton 0, Gibb 0); seventh day, England 253-1 (Gibb 78, Edrich 107); eighth day, no play; ninth day, England 496-3 (Hammond 58, Paynter 24).

The Records

- The timeless Test is the longest first-class match played. It lasted nine playing days (rain prevented any play on the eighth day) and was spread over 12 days in all (3–14 March). There were 43 hours and 16 minutes of playing time.
- The 1,981 runs are the most recorded in a Test match.
- A record number of balls – 5,447 (680.7 overs) – were bowled in the match; the new ball was taken 12 times.
- England's second-innings total of 654 for five is the highest fourth-innings score in a Test.
- The second-wicket stand of 280 between Paul Gibb and Bill Edrich was a record partnership for any wicket in England–South Africa Tests. It remains the highest second-wicket partnership between the two countries.
- Edrich became the first Englishman to score a double-century in the second innings of a Test.
- Gibb's 120 was the slowest Test century scored by an Englishman. He reached his 100 in 362 minutes.

- Dudley Nourse reached his century (103) in 364 minutes and was the slowest by a South African in a Test.
- South Africa's aggregate of 1,011 runs was their highest in a Test.
- England's aggregate of 970 runs was their most in a Test against South Africa.
- Pieter van der Bijl's 125 in 428 minutes was the longest Test innings by a South African against England (the record for the longest innings by a South African was held by Charlie Frank, who hit 152 in 512 minutes against Australia in 1921). Van der Bijl spent 658 minutes at the crease in all – just two minutes under 11 hours.
- He was also the first South African to score a century and a 90 in the same Test.
- South Africa became only the second side to score more than 450 in both innings of a Test.
- There were 16 innings of over 50 in the match – no Test had previously produced as many.
- Nine of those half-centuries were recorded by South Africans – a record for the country.
- South Africa's first-innings total of 530 was their highest Test score.
- It was also the longest, at 13 hours, in Tests played between the two countries.

- Ronnie Grieveson's 75 during South Africa's first innings was the highest score by a wicketkeeper in his maiden Test innings.
- Hedley Verity's 766 balls (95.6 overs) were the most delivered by any bowler in a Test.
- Norman Gordon's 738 balls (92.2 overs) remain the most by a fast bowler in a Test.
- The £3,640 receipts from the first five days of the timeless Test were a record for Kingsmead.
- Stumps were drawn before time on eight consecutive days – on seven occasions for bad light and once for rain.
- Walter Hammond equalled Don Bradman's record when he scored his 21st Test century – 140 – in England's second innings.

MCC in South Africa 1938–39

List of 13 provincial matches played on tour:

Western Province Country District v MCC at the Strand, Cape Town, 8–9 November 1938: MCC 589-8dec (E. Paynter 193, W. Hammond 106, B. Valentine 69, L. Hutton 68, H. Verity 66no; J. Sleigh 5-161). Western Province County District: 140 (Verity 4-26, T. Goddard 4-39) & 107 (W. Edrich 4-13, Verity 3-29). MCC won by an innings and 342 runs.

Western Province v MCC at Newlands, Cape Town, 12–15 November: Western Province 174 (Edrich 4-10, K. Farnes 3-32) & 169 (A. Ralph 61no; Farnes 7-38, D. Wright 3-64). MCC: 276 (H. Bartlett 91no) & 69-2. MCC won by eight wickets.

Griqualand West v MCC at Kimberley Athletic Club, Kimberley, 19–22 November: MCC 676 (Paynter 158, Hutton 149, N. Yardley 142; J. McNally 5-154). Griqualand West 114 (Verity 7-22) & 273 (A. Steyn 65, F. Nicholson 61; Verity 4-44, Goddard 3-64). MCC won by an innings and 289 runs.

Orange Free State v MCC at the South African Railways Ground, Bloemfontein, 26–28 November: Orange Free State 128 (L. Wilkinson 5-10, Wright 5-81) & 260 (S. Coen 61; Verity 7-75). MCC: 412-6dec (Yardley 142no, Bartlett 100; H. Sparks 4-89). MCC won by an innings and 24 runs.

Natal v MCC at Kingsmead, Durban, 3–5 December: Natal 307 (R. Harvey 92, W. Wade 56; Verity 3-49, Wright 3-81) & 30-0. MCC 458 (Hammond 122, Hutton 108, Edrich 98; E. Dalton 6-116). Match drawn.

North-Eastern Transvaal v MCC at Berea Park, Pretoria, 10–13 December: North-Eastern Transvaal 161 (L. Brown 75; Wilkinson 5-24, Goddard 3-49) & 142 (Verity 4-20). MCC: 379-6dec (Paynter 102, Valentine 100, Hutton 66). MCC won by an innings and 76 runs.

Transvaal v MCC at the Wanderers, Johannesburg, 16–19 December: Transvaal 428-8dec (B. Mitchell 133, K. Viljoen 97, A. Langton 58; Wilkinson 4-74, Farnes 4-93) & 174-2 (S. Curnow 51). MCC: 268 (L. Ames 109; E. Davies 6-82). Match drawn.

Eastern Province v MCC, St George's Park, Port Elizabeth, 7–9 January, 1939: Eastern Province 172

(A. Coy 54no; Farnes 5-58, Wright 4-45) & 111 (Wright 4-39, R. Perks 3-29). MCC: 518-6dec (Hutton 202, Paynter 99, Hammond 52, P. Gibb 51). MCC won by an innings and 235 runs.

Border v MCC at the Recreation Ground, East London, 13–16 January: Border 121 (Wright 4-34, Wilkinson 3-15) & 275 (R. Evans 88, D. Dowling 61; Wilkinson 4-63, Perks 3-86). MCC: 320 (Yardley 126, Wright 61; R. Chapman 4-60) & 79-1 (Edrich 50no). MCC won by nine wickets.

Combined Transvaal Xl v MCC at the Wanderers, Johannesburg, 27–30 January: Combined Transvaal XI 304 (Mitchell 83, Viljoen 76; Goddard 4-71) & 220-2 (A. Melville 107, E. Rowan 67no). MCC 434 (Hutton 148, Hammond 79, Valentine 71; S. Viljoen 6-91, E. Newson 3-78). Match drawn.

Rhodesia v MCC at Queen's Ground, Bulawayo, 4–7 February: MCC 307-5dec (Hutton 145, Paynter 53). Rhodesia: 242 (P. Mansell 62; Wright 4-64, Wilkinson 3-66). Match drawn.

Rhodesia v MCC at Salisbury Sports Club, 10–13 February: MCC 180 & 174-2 (Edrich 101no). Rhodesia: 96 (Goddard 6-38) & 95-6. Match drawn.

Natal v MCC at Alexandra Park, Pietermaritzburg, 25–28 February: Natal 295 (Dalton 110, D. Nourse 67; Wilkinson 4-43, Perks 3-56) & 219 (Wright 6-55). MCC: 407 (Edrich 150, Ames 62; J. Ellis 3-93) & 110-1 (Hutton 53no). MCC won by nine wickets.

Western Province v MCC at Newlands, Cape Town, 11–14 March: match cancelled (timeless Test still in progress).

Notes

One

1   England invariably appointed their captain for a home series on a Test-by-Test basis.
2   The Gentlemen's victory, by 133 runs, was only their second in this fixture at Lord's since the First World War.
3   Woodrooffe was true to his word but, according to *Time* magazine on 23 May 1938, the 'hat' he ate was in fact a cake in the shape of one.
4   Bartlett replaced the Kent batsman Arthur Fagg, who declined his invitation because of ill health. Two other players, 'Gubby' Allen and the opening batsman Charlie Barnett, had announced their unavailability earlier during the season. The Nottinghamshire batsman Joe Hardstaff was a surprise omission, and some reports suggest that his exclusion amounted to an oversight on the part of Pelham Warner and the selectors.

Two

1   There were 39 matches in all, including a trip to the Hague where they played a fixture against the Netherlands on a matting wicket. Moreover, they returned home with a profit of some £18,000, making it easily the most successful tour undertaken by South Africa at that time.
2   It was a feat the Springboks would not manage again in England until 1965, when Peter van der Merwe's side won the series 1–0 on what proved to be the last visit by a South African touring side to Britain for 29 years.

3   Cameron's electrifying 90 was his highest Test score. In 26 Tests he hit 1,239 runs at an average of just over 30, completing 39 catches and 12 stumpings.

4   Duffus also made a brief appearance as a player on the tour after injuries had reduced the Springboks to only 11 fit players for the match against Glamorgan at Swansea on 3–6 August. When Herbert Wade damaged his hand and had to go off during Glamorgan's second innings, he recalled, 'a message was sent to me in the press box, and with borrowed flannels and a good deal of apprehension I went out to field'. Duffus made an instant impression, catching the opening batsman A. H. Dyson at slip off the bowling off Bruce Mitchell – a dismissal that, according to *Wisden*, 'initiated a South African recovery'. The tourists went on to win by 96 runs.

Three

1   In David Thurlow's *Ken Farnes: Diary of an Essex Master*, Farnes wrote that Hutton was unconscious for fully 15 minutes.

2   Gibb played so little cricket during the first weeks of the tour, Farnes observed, that he had been virtually reduced to the role of 'a picnic member'. Bartlett, with a buccaneering century against Orange Free State and an undefeated 91 against Western Province already to his name, would have had good reason to feel hard done by.

3   The match was the 60th played between the two countries, 50 years since their first meeting in March 1889.

4   The 22,000 eclipsed the 18,000 attendance set during the first Test between South Africa and Australia at the Wanderers in December 1935.

5   Swanton revealed in a *Sort of a Cricket Person* in 1972 that the BBC were paying him £126 for 20 broadcasts to commentate on the Tests. As he admitted, it was hardly

a lavish reward, 'though in line no doubt with BBC scales of payment in the thirties'. However, because of the unforeseen longevity of the timeless Test – he completed 10 sessions on air during the game – he was able to show 'a small profit on the enterprise' at the conclusion of the tour.

6   Yardley wrote in *Cricket Campaigns* that this was by no means the last of Gibb's escapades in his Ford. The car, he added, 'became quite famous – or infamous – before the tour was over. But, as Paul has threatened my life if I print them, I am afraid you will have to be content with just this sample'.

7   The South African selectors refused to panic after the defeat in Durban and made only two changes to the side for the fourth Test in Johannesburg. Ronnie Grieveson replaced Billy Wade behind the stumps, while the fast bowler Eric Davies – who spilled 106 runs from only 15 overs in the third Test – made way for his fellow Transvaaler and new-ball bowler, 'Bob' Newson.

Four

1   Pollock, in the *Daily Express*, reported that Van der Bijl used a special short-handled bat.

2   The matter clearly rankled with Farnes, who wrote a year later in *Tours and Tests* that, 'I am still ready to receive the £6,000 or more . . .'

3   Arthur William 'Dave' Nourse (1879–1948) was born in Croydon, Surrey, but went to South Africa with the army as a 17-year-old drummer in the West Riding Regiment and liked the country so much he decided to stay on. *Wisden* explained that he was known for so long as 'Dave' that he adopted it as his middle name instead of William. A hard-as-nails left-handed batsman, medium-paced swing bowler and exceptional slip fielder, he scored 2,234

runs in 45 consecutive Tests, including 11 fifties but only one century – 111 against Australia at Johannesburg in 1921. He toured the country of his birth on three occasions, making his last Test appearance at The Oval in 1924, and continued to play first-class cricket until he was 57. He scored 14,216 first-class runs, hitting a career-best 304 for Natal against Transvaal in the 1919–20 Currie Cup.

Five

1   The former Oxford University and Somerset pace bowler Robert Charles 'Crusoe' Robertson-Glasgow was some 6,000 miles away in England while the timeless Test was in progress, though you might never have known. However, as he pointed out in his notes on the match in the 1940 edition of *Wisden*, he was indebted to the benefit of Swanton's observations on it, and he simply furnished the colour – a task for which he was extraordinarily well equipped.

2   In the words of *Wisden*, Crisp was 'one of the most extraordinary men ever to play Test cricket'. He played in nine games for South Africa, between 1935–36, and he is the only bowler to have taken four wickets in four balls twice in first-class cricket. Among his many adventures he founded *Drum*, a radical magazine for the black population of South Africa, but it was his war exploits for which he is most revered. As *Wisden* wrote, 'He was an outstanding but turbulent tank commander, fighting his own personal war against better-armoured Germans in Greece and North Africa. He had six tanks blasted from under him in a month and was awarded the Distinguished Service Order for great gallantry. However, he annoyed authority so much that General Montgomery intervened personally and prevented him being given a

Bar a year later; his second honour was downgraded to an MC.' He died in Colchester, Essex, aged 82 in 1994, with, so it was said, a copy of *Sporting Life* on his lap, having just lost a £20 bet.

Six

1 Harold Geoffrey 'Tuppy' Owen-Smith (1909–1990) was a supremely gifted all-round sportsman. Although he made only five appearances for South Africa, all against England in 1929, he created a lasting impression as a dashing strokemaker, hitting 129 in the third Test at Headingley and scoring 252 runs in the series at 42.00. He also won cricket, rugby and boxing blues at Oxford and played 10 rugby internationals for England as an attacking full-back, captaining them on three occasions. He qualified at St Mary's Hospital in London as a doctor of medicine and returned to South Africa, where he was a general practitioner for many years. He was only 30 in 1939 and there is no doubt his presence would have added considerably to the batting strength of the South Africans. Louis Duffus suggests that he had made himself available to the selectors for the timeless Test, but was passed over.

2 Edrich, Rowan and Gordon were said to be regular frequenters of the Athlone Gardens nightclub during the timeless Test. Gordon recalled that one spectator, exasperated by the ease with which England appeared to be heading towards victory on the last day, shouted at the South African fielders, 'The match wasn't lost at Kingsmead, fellas, it was lost at Athlone Gardens the night before.'

3 William Henry Ferguson (1880–1957) made what he thought would be his final and 41st tour in 1953–54, with New Zealand in South Africa, but was coaxed out of

retirement three years later to accompany the West Indies to England. It was on tour there, *Wisden* recorded, that 'a fall at a hotel in August prevented him from finishing it and he spent some time in hospital, returning home only two days before his death'. Earlier in 1957 he had been presented with the British Empire Medal for his services to the Commonwealth. The MCC and South Africa, he always maintained, were the most generous of his many employers, regularly awarding him a £25 bonus at the completion of a tour. The Australian board treated its fellow countryman only to 'a letter of thanks'.

4   Swanton claimed there was 'some slight evidence' to support the official view that flying was too dangerous a means of travel for MCC's players. The plane they would have flown on if the timeless Test was extended into an 11th day had to be dug out of the sand after landing at Mossel Bay on its way to Cape Town. 'I know because I was on it,' he wrote, 'as also was Walter Hammond . . .'

Seven

1   Douglas Alexander, writing for *Cricinfo* in 2009, explained that Melville became 'so accustomed to the daily routine of breakfast at their seafront hotel, followed by a drive to the ground, that [on the second rest day of the timeless Test] he looked around the dining room surprised to see no team-mates in sight. "They'll be late for the ground if they don't hurry," he complained to a waiter. "But it's Sunday, sir," the smiling waiter replied'. Alexander added that Melville gave his complimentary tickets to an Imperial Airways flying-boat crew before the start of the Test: 'They watched the first day's play and, on reaching Britain after a four-day flight across Africa and the Mediterranean, handed their tickets to the new crew flying south. They arrived in Durban another four days later, yet still in time to watch the end of the match.'

2　Campbell achieved his last land speed record of 301.13mph at Bonneville salt-flats in Utah in 1935, and set another world record, this time on water, when he touched 141.44mph on Coniston Water in the Lake District in 1939.

3　Hutton described Smuts as a 'gentle, noble man' but admitted that, when 'I asked him the question uppermost in everybody's mind about the possibility of war, he did not prove himself to be much of a prophet . . .'

4　Graeme Pollock, Barry Richards and Mike Procter, to name but a few South African luminaries, first came to notice in the Nuffield Schools Week.

Eight

1　As they had been since their succession to Test status 11 years earlier, they were captained by a white West Indian, in this case Rolph Grant, a batsman who had struggled to hold down a first-team place in the Cambridge University XI. Constantine and Headley, both highly attuned, tactically shrewd cricketers in their own right, were not considered for the role, though they were the natural candidates. Instead they had to shoulder the burden of carrying the team, in terms of their playing skills, on the field. As such, the white West Indian was easily identifiable with the English amateur.

2　The SS *Athenia* was the first British ship to be sunk during World War Two. The sinking was condemned as a war crime, and 128 passengers and crew lost their lives.

Epilogue

1　Group captain Albert John (Jack) Holmes died suddenly at his home in Burwash, Sussex, aged 50, after a heart attack on 21 May 1950. He returned to the RAF during the war when he was awarded the Air Force Cross in

1940, receiving a Bar to the decoration two years later. In 208 first-class matches for Sussex and MCC, Holmes scored 6,282 runs at 21.22 with a highest score of 133. He was chairman of selectors for four years after the war but had to resign in 1950 because of ill health. 'His genial personality made him very popular and contributed largely to his success as manager of the MCC team in South Africa in 1938–39,' *Wisden* wrote. He made one appearance as a player on tour, scoring three not out against Orange Free State in Bloemfontein.

Bibliography

Books

Alfred L., *Testing Times: The Story of the Men Who Made SA Cricket*, Spearhead Press, Cape Town, 2003

Ames L., *Close of Play*, Stanley Paul, London, 1953

Barker R., *Ten Great Innings*, Chatto & Windus, London, 1964

Bassano B., *MCC in South Africa 1938–39*, J. W. McKenzie, Surrey, 1997

Bateman A. & Hill J. (ed.), *The Cambridge Companion to Cricket*, Cambridge University Press, Cambridge, 2011

Batchelor D., *The Book of Cricket*, Collins, London, 1952

Birley D., *A Social History of English Cricket*, Aurum Press, London, 1999

Bradman D., *Farewell to Cricket*, Hodder & Stoughton, London, 1950

Cardus N. & Hart-Davis R. (ed.), *The Essential Neville Cardus*, Jonathan Cape, London, 1949

Duffus L., *Cricketers of the Veld*, Sampson Low, Marston & Co, London, 1946

Duffus L., *Play Abandoned*, Bailey Bros & Swinfen, London, 1969

Edrich W., *Cricket Heritage*, Stanley Paul, London, 1948

Farnes K., *Tours and Tests*, Lutterworth Press, London, 1940

Ferguson W. & Jack D. R., *Mr Cricket: The Autobiography of W. H. Ferguson*, Nicholas Kaye, London, 1957

Fingleton J. H., *Cricket Crisis*, Cassell, London, 1946

Foot D., *Wally Hammond: The Reasons Why*, Robson Books, London, 1996

Frindall W. (ed.), *The Wisden Book of Test Cricket: 1877-1977*, Wisden, London, 2010

Gardiner J., *The Thirties: An Intimate History*, Harper Press, London, 2010

Gibson A., *The Cricket Captains of England*, Cassell, London, 1979

Hammond W. R., *Cricket My Destiny*, Stanley Paul, London, 1946

Hayter P. (ed.), *Great Tests Recalled*, Bloomsbury, London, 1990

Hayter P. (ed.), *Cricket Heroes*, Bloomsbury, London, 1990

Hayter R. (ed.), *The Best of The Cricketer: 1921–1981. The Sixtieth Anniversary Selection*, Cassell, London, 1981

Heald, T., *Denis Compton: The Authorised Biography*, Aurum Press, London, 2006

Hill A., *Les Ames*, Christopher Helm, London, 1990

Hill A., *Bill Edrich: A Biography*, Andre Deutsch, London, 1994

Hill A., *Hedley Verity: Portrait of a Cricketer*, Kingswood Press, Surrey, 1986

Howat G., *Len Hutton: The Biography*, Heinemann Kingswood, London, 1988

Howat G., *Walter Hammond*, George Allen & Unwin, London, 1984

Howat G., *Cricket's Second Golden Age: The Hammond–Bradman Years*, Hodder & Stoughton, 1989

Hutton L., *Cricket Is My Life*, Hutchinson, London, 1949

Hutton L., *Fifty Years in Cricket*, Stanley Paul, London, 1984

Bibliography

Knowles R., *South Africa Versus England: A Test Cricket History*, New Holland, London, 1995

Martin-Jenkins C., *The Complete Who's Who of Test Cricketers*, Orbis, London, 1980

Mason R., *Walter Hammond*, Hollis & Carter, 1962, London

McGlew J. & Chesterfield T., *South Africa's Cricket Captains: from Melville to Wessels*, Southern Book Publishers, Johannesburg, 1994

Mortimer G., *Fields of Glory: The Extraordinary Lives of 16 Warrior Sportsmen*, André Deutsch, London, 2001

Moyes A. G., *A Century of Cricketers*, Angus & Robertson, London, 1950

Nourse D., *Cricket in the Blood*, Hodder & Stoughton, London, 1949

Paynter E., *Cricket All the Way*, A. Richardson, Leeds, 1962

Pollock W., *Talking About Cricket*, Victor Gollancz, London, 1941

Pugh M., *We Danced All Night: A Social History of Britain Between the Wars*, Vintage, London 2009

Stern J. & Williams M. (ed.), *The Essential Wisden: An Anthology of Wisden Cricketers' Almanack*, Bloomsbury, London, 2013

Swanton E. W., *The World of Cricket*, Michael Joseph, London, 1966; reprint Collins, London, 1980

Swanton E. W., *Sort of a Cricket Person*, Collins, London, 1972

Swanton E. W., *Follow On*, Collins, London, 1977

Thurlow D., *Ken Farnes: Diary of an Essex Master*, The Parrs Wood Press, Manchester, 2000

Valentine B., *Cricket's Dawn That Died*, Breedon Books, Derby, 1991

Ward A., *Cricket's Strangest Matches*, Robson Books, London, 1999

Waters C., *10 For 10: Hedley Verity and the Story of Cricket's Greatest Bowling Feat*, Bloomsbury, London, 2014

Wilde S., *Wisden Cricketers of the Year: A Celebration of Cricket's Greatest Players*, John Wisden and Co, London, 2013

Winder R., *The Little Wonder: The Remarkable History of Wisden*, Bloomsbury, London, 2013

Yardley N., *Cricket Campaigns*, Stanley Paul, London, 1950

General

Wisden Cricketers' Almanack

Newspapers, magazines

Birmingham Post
Daily Express
Daily Mail
Daily Mirror
Daily Telegraph
Daily Tribune
Gloucester Citizen
Gloucester Echo
Guardian
Hastings & St Leonards Observer
Illustrated London News
Independent
Leeds Mercury
Liverpool Daily Post
London Evening Standard
Manchester Evening News

Natal Mercury
Natal Daily News
Portsmouth Evening News
Rand Daily Mail
SA Cricket magazine
SA Times
Sheffield Independent
The Spectator
Star (London)
Star (Johannesburg)
The Times
Western Mail
Yorkshire Post

Websites
www.britishnewspaperarchive.co.uk
www.cricketarchive.com
www.cricketcountry.com
www.espncricinfo.com
www.sahistory.org.za
www.test-cricket-tours.co.uk
www.trove.nla.gov.au

Acknowledgments

Many thanks to Bloomsbury Publishing, especially to Charlotte Atyeo and Holly Jarrald for all their hard work and patience, and to Ian Preece for his excellent copy-editing. Thanks to my agent, Charlie Viney, for his continued support and belief in this project. I am indebted to Roger Mann for helping me with a book for the third time by supplying photographs and information from his wonderful collection; as always, his positive thoughts were much appreciated. Thanks to David Studham and Trevor Ruddell at the MCG library for all their assistance, and for successfully tracking down one particularly elusive book for me; and to Roger Page and Charles Davis, also in Australia, for their valuable contributions. I am most grateful to Neil Robinson at Lord's for providing me with a fascinating glimpse into Bill Ferguson's scorebook of the 1938–39 tour. A special thanks also to my New Zealand family, particularly Jean Meyer for being the best host and office manager that a writer could wish for. Finally, all my thanks to Sharon, for everything. As ever, I could not have done it without you.

Index